SHAKES & SMOOTHIES

SHAKES & SMOOTHIES

75 IRRESISTIBLE RECIPES FOR BLENDED DRINKS, SHOWN
STEP BY STEP IN MORE THAN 300 STUNNING PHOTOGRAPHS

JOANNA FARROW

southwater

This edition is published by Southwater an imprint of Anness Publishing Ltd
Blaby Road, Wigston, Leicestershire LE18 4SE; info@anness.com

www.southwaterbooks.com; www.annesspublishing.com

If you like the images in this book and would like to investigate using them for publishing,
promotions or advertising, please visit our website www.practicalpictures.com for more information.

A CIP catalogue record for this book is available from the British Library.

Publisher: Joanna Lorenz
Managing Editor: Judith Simons
Editor: Clare Gooden
Assistant Editor: Lindsay Kaubi
Photographers: Gus Filgate and Craig Robertson, with additional pictures by Janine Hosegood and Simon Smith
Stylist: Helen Trent
Designer: Nigel Partridge
Cover Designer: Balley Design Associates
Additional Recipes: Susannah Blake, Nicola Graimes and Jane Milton
Production Controller: Wendy Lawson

Previously published as part of a larger volume, *Juicing, Smoothies & Blended Drinks*

PUBLISHER'S NOTE
Although the advice and information in this book are believed to be accurate and true at the time of going
to press, neither the authors nor the publisher can accept any legal responsibility or liability for any errors
or omissions that may have been made nor for any inaccuracies nor for any loss, harm or injury that
comes about from following instructions or advice in this book.

NOTES
Bracketed terms are intended for American readers.
For all recipes, quantities are given in both metric and imperial measures and, where appropriate,
measures are also given in standard cups and spoons.
Follow one set, but not a mixture, because they are not interchangeable.
Standard spoon and cup measures are level.1 tsp = 5ml, 1 tbsp = 15ml, 1 cup = 250ml/8fl oz
Australian standard tablespoons are 20ml. Australian readers should use 3 tsp in place of 1 tbsp for measuring
small quantities of gelatine, flour, salt, etc.
American pints are 16fl oz/2 cups. American readers should use 20fl oz/2.5 cups in place of 1 pint when measuring liquids.
Medium (US large) eggs are used unless otherwise stated.
The very young, elderly and those in ill-health or with a compromised immune system are advised against consuming
juices or blends that contain raw eggs.
Always check the manufacturer's instructions before using a blender
or food processor to crush ice.

CONTENTS

Introduction

Smoothies, shakes and blends have become extremely popular in recent years. They fit neatly into hectic modern lives, enabling you to incorporate healthy habits into your everyday routines. The main advantage of smoothies is that they are easy to make, quick, convenient and packed with rejuvenating, healing and revitalizing nutrients. On top of all this, they are also delicious, and a luxurious blended drink can feel like a real treat.

Health Benefits

While you can buy ready-made smoothies, nothing quite beats the taste of a blend made at home. Freshly made drinks are also a more potent source of nutrients and certain combinations have specific health benefits. If you drink fresh blends on a regular basis, you'll enjoy clearer skin, better energy levels and balanced overall health. It is also well known that the antioxidants found in fruits and vegetables work most effectively when they are consumed together, and blending encourages precisely this.

Combinations of specific different ingredients can be used to emphasize particular flavours or effects in the same way that you would in cooking – sweet and sour, savoury and spicy, warming or cooling – but you can afford to be

Above: Fresh flavours are whizzed up into nutrient-packed blends in minutes.

more adventurous than you might be with conventionally prepared foods. The flavours of a fruit or vegetable often taste much better than when the produce is cooked or even served raw. For instance, you may not particularly like celery as a vegetable, but blend it with pear and ginger and you get a completely different, more complex and utterly delicious taste sensation.

Even if you feel like going off the rails and indulging in extra ingredients, such as chocolate, alcohol or coffee, the very fact that the smoothie is based on fresh fruits and vegetables means that you are still getting a wonderful boost of vitamins, antioxidants and minerals – healthy in anyone's book.

Preparing smoothies and blends also has a psychological benefit. The very act of making a smoothie can make you feel good – you will feel you are nurturing and pampering yourself – and in addition, by using lots of fresh

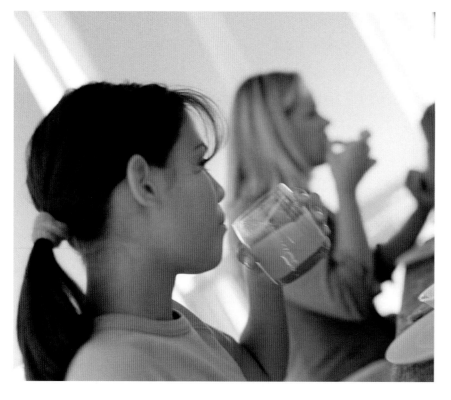

Left: Let children get involved in blending and watch them reap the benefits.

natural ingredients you will boost your own health and the health of your family. Smoothies are great fun to make and to share: encourage your children to invent concoctions and join in the preparation, or share a blend or a smoothie instead of coffee with a friend.

The History of Smoothies, Blends and Shakes

In the 19th century, doctors and naturopaths were using fresh fruit and vegetable blends and juices to improve the health of their patients. Many well-known pioneers were responsible for researching and creating the wealth of knowledge and evidence we now have about the therapeutic properties of blends and juices. People such as Dr Kellogg, Father Kniepp, Dr Max Bircher-Bener and Dr Max Gerson all helped to popularize the notion of the "juice cure".

However, there is evidence to suggest that blending and juicing is even older than this in the ancient practices of wine and scrumpy (apple cider) making. After extracting the fresh

Below: The process of making blended drinks is as enjoyable as drinking them.

fruit juices, fermenting them into alcohol was simply a way of preserving the raw ingredients – and in those days drinking alcohol was safer than drinking water, which was often contaminated. The healing power of certain foods was even recognized by Hippocrates who said "Let food be your medicine." Indeed, since time immemorial, food, water and healing herbs have been the cornerstones of the healing arts.

The modern concept of blending drinks and making smoothies probably began with mixed drinks such as cocktails. For the more virtuous and health-conscious among us, however, non-alcoholic blends and smoothies have always sat comfortably alongside the bar choice.

We are going through a change in how we involve ourselves in our health. Reliance on prepared and fast foods has given way to a re-emergence of interest in healthy eating messages – the most familiar of these is that we need to eat five portions of fruit and vegetables every day. One convenient way of achieving this, in the context of our modern, fast-paced lives, is to embrace health drinks as easy-to-make

Above: Raw ingredients that can be juiced provide all the vitamins and minerals that you need to stay healthy.

snacks, quick breakfasts and fast energy boosters. The introduction of advanced kitchen technology, such as blenders, food processors and juicers, has made the preparation of blends and juices quick and easy.

In recent years, we have become more and more interested in natural ways of improving our health – echoing the thoughts and practices of the pioneering enthusiasts of earlier centuries. In addition to their more general health-boosting properties, smoothies and blends are also used for specific cleansing and detoxing, for helping speed recovery from illness and as part of anti-ageing regimes. There is also a school of thought that maintains that blends can help prevent some cancers, although this has yet to be proven. Nevertheless, freshly made fruit and vegetable smoothies and blends provide many of the essential vitamins and minerals that are vital for a long and healthy life.

It is not often that something so healthy also tastes so good and is a pleasure to incorporate into daily life. Perhaps this is why blended drinks, smoothies and shakes are standing the test of time and gaining popularity around the world.

the art of blending

Learn about blending techniques. Discover the best equipment to use for each drink, which ingredients work well together and how to get the most nutrients from your blend.

Getting equipped

For successful blending and delicious smoothies, you will need some basic equipment. The chances are that you will have several items such as a food processor or a blender already, but there are some more specialist items available that will make the job easier, quicker and much more fun.

Food Processors

These multi-functional machines are excellent for blending and juicing combinations and if you are producing large quantities. They comprise a main bowl and a variety of attachments, some of which are supplied with the original purchase, while others can be bought individually. For making smoothies and blends, the most important attachments are:
• A strong blade that blends medium-hard or soft fruit and vegetables.
• A centrifugal juicing attachment that turns your food processor into a juicer.
• A citrus press attachment.
• Whisking attachments.
• Ice crushing attachments.

Below: Your food processor can be used to blend soft fruits into purées.

Right: Blenders turn soft fruits into delicious smoothies and milkshakes.

Blenders

These feature a plastic or glass jug (pitcher) placed on top of a motorized base, which powers blades inside the jug. Blenders work best with soft fruit, such as bananas, peaches and berries, to which you add a liquid ingredient, such as water, milk or juice, to create delicious smoothies and shakes. Some can also be used to crush ice, but always check the instructions.

Electric Wand

These handheld electric mixers are good for no-fuss blending. Some models come with a variety of attachments for blending and whisking. You need to use an electric wand with a deep bowl, or a flask (which is sometimes supplied). If you are going to blend regularly you will find it much more practical to buy a proper blender, although wands can blend soft fruit and liquid, syrup or powdered ingredients well. Creamy whipped toppings can be made with the whisk attachment.

Other Useful Equipment

Chopping board Buy a big chopping board that will accommodate large quantities of fruits and vegetables. Plastic boards are easier to keep clean than wooden ones. To clean chopping boards, scrub with washing-up liquid (dishwashing detergent), then allow them to air dry – drying with a cloth often leads to recontamination. To avoid contamination, use a separate chopping board for meat.
Vegetable scrubbing brush Use a firm brush to remove dirt from your vegetables, particularly root vegetables, as an alternative to peeling.
Zester A zester is extremely useful for grating rind and adding intense citrus flavour. The row of holes at the top of the zester shaves off thin shreds of rind, leaving the bitter white pith behind.

Above: Ice cream scoops are available in many different shapes and styles.

Above: Sieves can be used to strain thick blends or to remove large seeds.

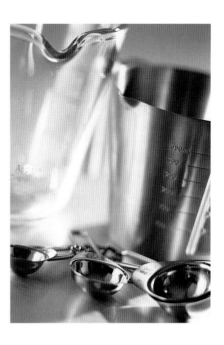

Above: For exact amounts, use a set of measuring jugs and spoons.

Canelle knife This tool has a tooth-like blade that pares off the rind in ribbons or julienne strips. Combined zester/canelle knives are also available.

Apple corer These make quick work of coring apples or pears before you blend them. Place over the core at the stem end and push down firmly right through the fruit, then twist slightly and pull out the core and pips. There is no need to core apples or pears if you are putting them through a juicer.

Sharp knife Make sure your knife is really sharp because this will make chopping much easier, and safer too.

Plastic spatula These are very handy for scraping thick blends out of a blender or food processor, and the plastic will not scratch or damage the equipment.

Left: Citrus zesters and canelle knives are useful for preparing fruit.

Cherry stoner This simple tool takes the hard work out of pitting cherries and makes it much quicker. The bowl of the implement has a hole through which the cherry stone is ejected when the fruit is pressed.

Melon baller Insert this small round scoop into the melon flesh and twist to remove neat balls of fruit. Melon balls can also be used to garnish.

Measuring jugs Available in either glass or plastic and in many different sizes, measuring jugs (pitchers) must have the measurements clearly marked for ease of use. It's worth buying a large measuring jug.

Sieve This can be useful when you want to strain juices to remove seeds and pips for fussy children, or if you just want a thinner juice.

Ice cream scoops These are useful for scooping ice cream, frozen yogurt or sorbet into milkshakes or smoothies. Choose from half-moon-shaped stainless-steel scoops with sleek steel handles, simple spoon-shaped scoops with metal handles or easy-grip moulded plastic handles, or brightly coloured plastic scoops with quick release levers. For smaller rounds of sorbet or frozen yogurt, try using a melon baller as a scoop.

Storage jug or vacuum flask Choose a storage jug (pitcher) with a close-fitting lid or place clear film (plastic wrap) over the opening before securing the lid. Covering the blend securely limits its exposure to oxygen and prevents oxidization. Even better, use a wide-necked vacuum flask.

Serving jugs and glasses Buy different shapes and colours and have some fun, contrasting them with the colour of the smoothie you are serving.

Above: From the top, a cherry stoner, an apple corer and a melon baller.

Blending and juicing techniques

For maximum freshness and flavour, prepare the fruit and vegetables directly before using.

TROUBLESHOOTING

If you experience any problems using a blender or food processor, the following may help.

The blend is too thick
Thin it using water or the juice of a watery fruit.

The blend is too pulpy
Strain the mixture through a sieve, using the back of a spoon.

The ingredients get stuck
Scrape down with a plastic spatula and mix all ingredients thoroughly.

Blenders and Food Processors

The preparation of fruit is the same for both types of equipment. The difference between them is the point at which you add liquid to the blend.

1 Fruits with inedible skins, such as bananas, mangoes and papayas, should be peeled.

2 Fruits with edible skins, such as peaches or plums, do not need to be peeled but should be washed thoroughly. If you prefer a juice with a finer, smoother texture, peel the fruits before blending.

3 Fruits with large stones (pits), cores or pips (seeds), such as mangoes, plums, cherries and apples, should be stoned (pitted), cored or seeded.

4 Fruits with tiny seeds, such as raspberries, strawberries or kiwis, can be used whole, and the seeds add texture and a pretty speckled effect. However, if you prefer a smooth drink, the pulp can be pushed through a fine sieve to remove the seeds.

5 When using berries and currants, remove the stalks and leaves and wash the fruit thoroughly. An easy way to detach, or string, redcurrants or blackcurrants from their stalks is to hold the bunch firmly at the top, then slowly draw a fork through the fruit.

6 To blend fruit in a food processor, place it in the bowl of the machine and process to a thick pulp. Add any liquid or creamy ingredient, such as water, fruit juice, milk or yogurt, and process again.

7 To blend fruit in a blender, it is important to add the liquid ingredients and the soft fruit at the same time, then process altogether, otherwise the blades will not be able to blend the fruits effectively.

8 If using a handheld electric wand, remember that this piece of equipment is not as powerful as other juicers or blenders. Use only very soft fruits, such as bananas, peaches and berries, as it cannot cope with anything firmer.

Citrus Juicers
1 First, cut the citrus fruit in half using a sharp knife.

2 To use a traditional handheld juicer, press the cut half over the cone of the juicer and, using an even pressure all round, twist the fruit to squeeze out as much juice as possible. The rim of the squeezer will catch any pips (seeds) but you may need a bowl to catch the juice.

3 To use a juicer with a citrus attachment or an electrically operated citrus juicer, firmly press the halved fruit over the spinning cone of the juicer. The motor will turn the cone under the fruit, and this will extract more juice than a handheld juicer would usually produce.

4 To use a manual hydraulic press, place a container under the juice nozzle to collect the juice (unless one is supplied as part of the juicer) and place the halved citrus fruit in the press. Pull the lever forwards to apply pressure and squeeze out the juice.

5 To use a centrifugal or masticating juicer, remove the citrus peel with a sharp knife (there is no need to worry about removing the pips or the white pith that remains). Cut the fruit into similar-sized chunks or break into segments, then press the fruit through the juicer funnel.

QUICK START TIPS
If you are impatient to get going, you can achieve some delicious instant results with one of these simple basic blends.

Banana and Berry Milkshake
1 banana
generous handful of strawberries, raspberries or other soft berries
1 glass cold milk or soya milk

Peel the banana and chop into chunks. Put all the ingredients in a blender or food processor. Blend, pour into a glass and serve.

Carrot and Apple Juice
2 large carrots
1 apple

Wash the carrots and apple, cut into chunks and push through a juicer. Spoon off any foam, if you prefer, and serve.

Lemon and Orange Refresher
1 orange
½ lemon
sparkling water
5ml/1 tsp sugar (optional)
ice cubes and/or fresh mint leaves

Juice the fruit in a juicer. Add the sparkling water and sugar, if using. Pour into a glass, add ice cubes and/or mint leaves, then serve.

Tomato and Pepper Boost
½ red (bell) pepper
150g/5oz tomatoes
juice of ½ lime
ice cubes

Soak the tomatoes in boiling water, then peel off the skin and chop into chunks. Halve the red pepper, remove the seeds and chop into similar-sized chunks. Add the pepper and tomatoes to a blender or food processor and blend well. Add a squeeze of lime juice and some ice cubes, then serve.

Serving and storing smoothies and blends

The ideal way to enjoy blends and smoothies is to drink them immediately. This way you benefit from the full flavour and nutritional benefits, because time and exposure to oxygen take their toll on the nutrient content of most prepared fruits and vegetables. For instance, when you make a blend with carrot juice, it is a bright orange colour, but if you leave it for an hour it will turn brown as it oxidizes. Likewise, the flesh of apples or avocados turns brown as it oxidizes and loses nutritional value.

Serving and Decorating Smoothies and Blends

There are many attractive and quirky ways to serve fresh drinks. With a little forethought and imagination, you can present friends and family with gorgeous-looking concoctions – whatever the occasion.

Adding ice Ice is a wonderful vehicle for serving, cooling and decorating drinks. Cubes are best for cooling drinks, and these can be decorated or flavoured in different ways. A handful of ice can be added to a drink, or you can add crushed ice to drinks in glasses to cool them quickly.

Juicy ice cubes Make cubes from orange, cranberry or diluted lime blends and juices in an ice-cube tray. These will create a rainbow effect in your drinks and will also alter the taste as they melt.

Right: Suspend sprigs of currants over your drinks for a stunning effect.

Fruit ice cubes Place raspberries or other small fruits in an ice-cube tray and add water.

Flower ice cubes Choose edible flowers that will be attractive when the ice has melted – rose petals, carnation pinks or borage flowers.

Fruit purée drizzle For a striped effect, pour fruit purée down the inside of glasses before adding the drink.

Sugar-rimmed glasses Moisten the rim of a glass with water, dip into grated lemon or lime zest and then into icing (confectioners') sugar.

Edible swizzle sticks These can be fun and celery sticks are a natural choice for savoury drinks. Finely slice one end of the stick then soak in iced water for about 15 minutes – a fanned out fringe will develop.

Fruit skewers Place fruit segments or currants on a skewer and use as a swizzle stick. Bruised lemon grass stalks, lavender or rosemary stems, or cinnamon sticks can also be used.

Glass decorations Place fruit slices on the rim of a glass or skewer small pieces of fruit on to cocktail sticks (toothpicks) and balance these across the tops of glasses. Experiment with herb leaves and pared citrus rind.

Ice lollies Fruit juices make healthy ice lollies (popsicles) for children. All you need is an inexpensive mould, available from kitchenware shops. This is a fun way to serve drinks at parties.

Storage of Blends

While it is definitely best to serve blends and smoothies when they are just freshly made, you may want to store them for one reason or another. Perhaps you have made too much to drink in one go, maybe you have a glut of berries or some other produce that you need to use up before it over-ripens, or you might simply want to take a juice or smoothie into work for a healthy mid-morning snack.

One way to minimize the oxidization of blends is to add some vitamin C. Either squeeze in a little fresh lemon or orange juice or add 2.5ml/½ tsp of powdered vitamin C, which is available from health food shops. Blends can then be stored in the refrigerator for a few hours and won't discolour – make sure you chill them as soon as possible after making.

Above: To make children's parties fun, try serving blends frozen into lollies.

To store a blend or smoothie pour it into a jar or jug (pitcher), filling it right to the brim. Seal with clear film (plastic wrap) or, alternatively, use a screw-top jug or vacuum flask.

Most blends can be frozen for use at a later date and this will preserve almost all of their full nutritional value. Try freezing different flavoured blends in ice-cube trays – the ice cubes can then simply be removed and added to drinks. Otherwise, try to freeze the blend in fairly small amounts (glassfuls). Any blended drink can be frozen successfully, but it is a good idea to make single ingredient base blends to freeze, because you can then add different flavourings when the blend is thawed. Make sure you label and date the containers clearly.

Buying produce

If you are really enthusiastic about making smoothies and blends you may want to bulk buy some of the basic ingredients. Carrots, apples, bananas, pineapples and oranges are often used as bases to which other ingredients are added. Additional ingredients, such as summer berries, are best used when really fresh and so should be blended on the day of purchase.

Freshness

The produce you use for smoothies and blends should be as fresh as possible to ensure that you will get the maximum nutrients from your drinks. It is not necessary to buy produce that looks perfect, but do avoid any that is bruised, damaged or overripe. Aim to buy fruit and vegetables that are in season if you can. By buying seasonally and locally, your produce will be bursting with health-boosting vitamins and minerals.

Ripeness

The riper the fruit, the more sugar it will contain and the sweeter it will be. It also means that the fruit contains more nutrients, especially if the produce has been ripened on the tree or plant. Fruits that are picked green and ripened in transit contain fewer nutrients.

Storage

All fruit and vegetables benefit from being stored in cool, dry conditions. However, if fruit is slightly underripe and too firm to be blended, find a sunny windowsill on which to ripen it for a couple of days. Avoid wrapping produce in plastic bags as it cannot breathe. Ideally you should store ingredients in individual bowls or trays – for instance, one for citrus fruits, one for bananas and one for onions – as they all have different ripening times and one item can affect another, leading to premature rotting.

Above: Buy produce that is ripe if you can, but if it is needs further ripening, simply leave it on a sunny windowsill.

Organic Produce

Food that is grown organically is slightly more expensive than regular produce, but there are some clear advantages in choosing it.

The levels of chemicals that you are exposed to via pesticides, fungicides and fertilizers will be significantly reduced if you choose organic produce. Advocates of organic fruit and vegetables also claim that they taste better because there is less water bulking out the produce. It is certainly true that if you taste an organic carrot and then compare it to the taste of a non-organic carrot, the former will usually have a more solid texture and a stronger, more intense carroty taste. This inevitably means that your blends will have more flavour, as there will be less water diluting the juice.

Even if you don't want to buy entirely organic produce, you may want to consider buying bulky base items, such as carrots and apples, from organic ranges.

Left: Organic fruits tend to contain less water so the taste is more intense, and they are exposed to fewer pesticides.

Above: It may be worth peeling the skin of non-organic produce, as this will remove any possible chemical residue.

Convenient Options

For convenience, and because you can't always find fresh produce out of season, it is worthwhile keeping some dried, frozen, canned and bottled fruits or vegetables to hand in your store cupboard (pantry). Use these as substitutes whenever you run out of a fresh ingredient or if you find that an ingredient is unavailable or out of season. Choose fruits that are preserved in unsweetened fruit juice in preference to syrup, as this is a more natural state. Dried fruit is also a useful standby, especially dried apricots, dates and figs.

Frozen fruit such as strawberries, raspberries, blueberries and bags of frozen mixed summer fruits work very well in smoothies and blended drinks. If blended straight from the freezer, they turn smoothies into deliciously chilled slushes and you will not need to add any additional ice.

Whole nuts and seeds (for grinding into blends or for sprinkling on top of drinks as decoration) and dry ingredients such as wheatgerm should be kept in airtight jars or packets and stored in the refrigerator to keep them fresh once opened. However, because of their high fat content, nuts and seeds will become rancid if you keep them for too long. Make sure you buy from a supplier with a rapid turnover and always check the use-by date on the packet before you add them to drinks.

IRRADIATION

Most herbs and spices are irradiated (treated with radiation to delay spoiling) but this is forbidden with organic produce. If you wish to avoid irradiated herbs and spices you need to buy organic.

GM CROPS

Genetically modified foods are a recent innovation. If you have concerns about this type of produce, buy organic fruit and vegetables. Be aware that most soya products are GM-based, so look in your local health food shop and choose products that state they contain "non-genetically modified soya" on the packet.

Below: To avoid genetically modified produce, buy organic – it is worth spending a little bit more.

Citrus fruit

In order to extract juice from citrus fruits for adding to blends and smoothies you you will need to use a citrus juicer. Oranges are available all year round and store well in cool, dry conditions. All citrus fruits are rich in vitamin C, and one large orange provides your recommended daily allowance (RDA). Oranges, tangerines, mandarins and other citrus fruits are also excellent sources of folic acid. As an alternative to using a citrus juicer, you could push the peeled fruit through a juicer to benefit from the fibre and pith. The pith is rich in two bioflavonoids, rutin and hesperidin, which aid the absorption of vitamin C and strengthen blood vessels. The rind is rich in limonene, which is very good for liver health. However, some people find that certain citrus fruits are too acidic for their digestive system.

Preparing and Juicing Citrus Fruits

To juice citrus fruits, you will need a citrus juicer (handheld, electric or hydraulic), a chopping board and a sharp knife. If you are going to use the rind, you will also need a scrubbing brush, soap or washing-up liquid (dishwashing detergent), and a grater.

Juicing The simplest way to juice citrus fruits is to cut them in half and squeeze out the juice using a handheld juicer or a reamer. A hydraulic citrus press or citrus attachment on a citrus juicer is more efficient, however, and will produce more juice. Press the cut fruit against the cone of the juicer. Peeled fruits can also be juiced in a juicer or blended using a food processor or blender.

Grating rind If you wish to use rind in a blend, choose a non-waxed organic fruit to avoid chemical residue or scrub the skin with a firm brush using a little soap, then rinse. Grate on the fine mesh of your grater or use a zester.

Oranges

These are generally sweet, although some have a sharper flavour than others. Always use eating oranges for blends; Seville (Temple) oranges are too bitter. Blood oranges are sweeter than regular oranges and produce a lovely ruby-red juice.

Oranges are used to make a base juice for blends, to which other juices can be added. To tone down the sweetness of orange juice, add grapefruit juice. Orange juice goes well with lots of other juices, particularly carrot, and also makes an excellent base for smoothies.

Therapeutic uses Orange juice is often used as a cold and flu remedy. It is rich in folic acid, which is good for cardiovascular health. It is recommended that women planning to conceive and those in the early stages of pregnancy have a good intake of folic acid in their diet (but supplements should also be taken to achieve the RDA at this time).

Grapefruits

Larger than oranges, grapefruits provide more juice. Their taste ranges from bitter/sour to sour/sweet. They add a mildly sour note to blended drinks and smoothies. Pink grapefruits are sweeter than yellow grapefruits.

Above: Vibrant pink grapefruits are sweeter than yellow ones.

Left: Oranges make a useful base for blended drinks.

Above: Refreshing clementines work as an effective digestive cleanser.

Therapeutic uses Grapefruit juice is thought to be useful in helping to lower cholesterol. It needs to be avoided if you are taking certain medications, particularly calcium-channel blockers and some chemotherapies. Consult your medical practitioner for advice.

Lemons and Limes

These fruits have a sour/bitter taste so are used only in small quantities. They are good with tomato juice, in cocktails such as mojitos, or in a hot toddy – honey and lemon juice with hot water (and brandy or whisky if you like). The delicious zesty flavour works well with almost any combination of ingredients.

Therapeutic uses Lemons have antiseptic and antibacterial properties, and are traditionally used to support liver and kidney health. They are an alkaline fruit and are often used to help calm digestive acid.

Right: Blends can be livened up with a fresh squeeze of lemon or lime juice.

Mandarins, Tangerines, Satsumas, Clementines and Tangelos

These are all different crosses of citrus fruit. They have individual mild, aromatic sweetness, which varies with the type of fruit. None is as tart as oranges. They make good bases for drinks and combine well with tropical fruit.

Therapeutic uses These fruits have similar properties to oranges and are also good digestive cleansers.

Other Citrus Fruits

Kumquat These can be fairly bitter, so combine them with intensely sweet ingredients, such as apricots. Slices of kumquat may also be used to decorate glasses.

GIVE ME FIVE!

Most governments agree that we need to eat five portions of fruit and vegetables a day, but many people are not sure what constitutes a "portion". Put simply, the daily total should come to 400g/14oz, so a portion is 80g/just under 3oz. A portion can be:

• one apple, one orange, one banana or another similar-sized fruit or vegetable
• two small fruits, such as tangerines or kiwi fruit
• half a large fruit, such as a grapefruit, or a generous slice of melon
• a small bowl of salad or fruit salad
• one cup of chopped vegetables
• one wine-glass full of fruit or vegetable juice (but remember that juice only counts towards one portion, so you can't drink juice all day and count it as five).

Note Potatoes do not count as a portion of vegetables because they are a starchy food.

Mineola This fruit is distinguished by a bump at its stem end. It has very few pips (seeds) and is wonderfully sweet, so is wonderfully tasty in blends.

Pomelos These are a type of orange with a sharp grapefruit flavour. Their slightly dry texture renders less juice than oranges, lemons or grapefruits, but their juice makes a good addition to mixed drinks that need sharpening.

Ugli fruit Named for its appearance, this fruit is delicious, mild, acid-sweet and juicy.

Orchard and stone fruit

Apples and pears are the classic orchard fruits and they make excellent base juices for blended drinks. Other benefits are that they are available year round and are relatively cheap. Other stone and orchard fruit, such as apricots, cherries and plums, are restricted to the summer season and tend to be more expensive, but they make a deliciously sweet addition to a drink. Store apples and pears in cool, dry conditions, but it is best to keep soft fruit in the refrigerator. All of these fruits are rich in vitamins and minerals, with apricots being particularly high in betacarotene – a source of vitamin A.

Preparing and Juicing Orchard and Stone Fruits

To extract juice from orchard and stone fruits, you will need either a juicer for hard fruits, such as apples, or a blender or food processor for softer fruits, such as peaches or plums. You will also need a chopping board and a sharp knife. A cherry stoner is useful for removing stones (pits) from cherries.

Hard fruits Apples, hard pears and quinces are best prepared with a juicer (centrifugal or masticating). Using a brush, scrub the skin with soap or washing-up liquid (dishwashing detergent) and water. Quarter the fruits and remove stems, but leave the core intact (although you can remove this if you prefer). Push the quarters through the juicer. Firmer peaches, nectarines or plums can also be put through a juicer, although the yield is much less than if blended. Halve or quarter these fruits and remove the stones.

Soft fruits Ripe apricots, cherries, peaches, nectarines, plums and greengages are best prepared in a blender or food processor as they produce a deliciously thick pulp. Halve or quarter these fruits, removing the stems and stones. There is no need to peel these fruits, though leaving the peel on will give the blend a thicker texture. If you do not peel the fruit, wash it thoroughly first.

Cherries These need to be pitted and this is most easily done using a cherry pitter.

To use a blender Place the fruit in the goblet and add your choice of liquid – water, juice, milk or milk substitute. Cover and select the appropriate speed. For a thicker consistency, add banana, yogurt or cream.

To use a food processor Place the prepared fruit in the bowl, cover and select the appropriate speed. The resulting pulp can be diluted to drinking consistency by adding water, a liquid juice such as apple or orange juice, milk or a milk substitute. If your food processor can crush ice, add some cubes at the end to create a lovely fruit "slush" drink.

CLASSIC COMBINATIONS

In the late summer and autumn, there is often a glut of locally grown orchard fruit or berries. Buy plenty and either freeze them for use later in the year, or juice them, taking advantage of some of these classic flavour combinations.

• **Apple and blackberry** – the sweetness of the apples offsets the tart blackberries perfectly.
• **Apple and carrot** – this juice is packed full of healthy nutrients.
• **Pear, melon and ginger** – the warmth of ginger complements the cool melon in this exotic blend.
• **Peach and apricot** – this thick blend can be thinned with sparkling mineral water.
• **Nectarine and cherry** – a delicious sweet blend that children will love.
• **Pear and cranberry** – this refreshing juice should be served with plenty of crushed ice.
• **Pear and apricot** – the thick, sweet apricot juice complements the subtle, aromatic flavour of pear.

Above: Apples can be very sweet, tangy or sour.

Apple

Depending on the type of apple, the taste will range from sweet to tart or sour. When making blended drinks and smoothies choose eating apples, not cooking or crab apples. Apples are available all year round, making them ideal as a base juice to which other ingredients can be added. Apple juice oxidizes quickly to a brown colour but a little lemon juice will slow this down.

Some classic flavour combinations are apple and cranberry, apple and blackcurrant, and apple and carrot. While it may seem that choosing sweet apples is best, sharper tasting eating varieties are often better, as juicing concentrates the sweetness. They also balance out sweeter ingredients – for instance, sharp green apples work well to counterbalance the flavour of intensely sweet watermelon.

Therapeutic uses Apples are a good all-round fruit. They contain malic acid, which aids digestion, and they are high in pectin, a soluble fibre that helps to lower cholesterol and may help in the treatment of constipation and diarrhoea. If you want to detox and generally clear out your system, apples are the perfect fruit. Some varieties are also very rich in vitamin C, so they can help to boost the immune system and stave off winter colds and flu.

Pears

These fruits have an aromatic scent and delicate flavour, which comes out particularly well when they are juiced. To fully enjoy their subtle flavour it is best not to mix them with other very strong tasting flavours, although they can be used to tone down the sometimes overwhelming flavours of cabbage and celery, for example.

Therapeutic uses This is another detoxifying fruit, which also provides an energizing boost. The levulose sugar in pears is more easily tolerated by diabetics than other sugars.

Apricots

If you can, choose tree-ripened fruit as the betacarotene levels increase by 200 per cent in the final ripening period. When blended, apricots produce a thick, rich pulp that is best when diluted with other more liquid juices such as cucumber, apple or carrot. Alternatively,

Above: Apricots make a deliciously thick and nutritious blend, perfect for a healthy breakfast.

you could thin the pulp with a splash of sparkling mineral water or add natural (plain) yogurt to make a delicious smoothie. Dried apricots can be prepared in a blender with some water.

Therapeutic uses Apricots are particularly rich in betacarotene, one of the most important antioxidants, while dried apricots are a useful source of iron, potassium and fibre.

Above: Aromatic pears make a subtle and refreshing juice.

Above: Fresh cherries have a short season so enjoy them while you can.

Cherries

Choose ripe, sweet cherries as they do not ripen further after picking. They should be plump and firm, but not hard. Cherries lend a rich, aromatic flavour to blended drinks and smoothies. Preparing them can be extremely time-consuming, and it helps if you have a cherry stoner to pit them. They are best used in small quantities with other blends and they turn juices and drinks a vibrant pinky-red colour. Cherry juice combines well with most other fruits and vegetables.

Therapeutic uses Powerhouses of the phyto (plant) nutrients proanthocyanins, which derive from their red colour, cherries have potent antioxidant characteristics. They also have painkilling abilities, which some people find particularly useful for relieving rheumatism. The pain relief characteristics can also be useful for alleviating headaches – a portion of 20 cherries is reputed to be the equivalent of one aspirin in terms of painkilling ability. Fresh cherries are also traditionally used to alleviate gout by helping to moderate uric acid levels. If you cannot find fresh cherries, the canned variety make a good substitute.

Peaches and Nectarines

These fruits produce similar thick, sweet juices, with peach juice being a little sweeter than that made with nectarines – but this difference is hardly noticeable once the juice has been blended.

Peaches have a fuzzy skin, which you may prefer to peel off before juicing, but this is not necessary. It is a bit of a waste putting peaches and nectarines

Above: Prunes add sweet flavour to a drink when whizzed up in a blender.

through a juicer as a much better yield can be achieved using a blender or food processor. This process retains the fibre of the fruit, resulting in a much thicker, fruit purée, which can then be thinned if you like. If a recipe calls for fresh apricots but it is the wrong season and you cannot find them, peaches or nectarines make a good substitute.

Therapeutic uses Rich in vitamin C, betacarotene and other antioxidants, peaches and nectarines are excellent for skin, lung and digestive health, and are also particularly good for your eyes. One fresh nectarine contains an adult's entire recommended daily allowance of vitamin C. These fruits are very easy to digest but have a gentle laxative and diuretic effect, so should always be eaten in moderation.

Above: Plums can be slightly sour if the fruit is underripe.

Left: Nectarines do not need to be peeled before blending, but the large stone must be removed.

Plums, Greengages, Damsons and Prunes

Plums and greengages have a sweet, refreshing taste, although some varieties, especially if unripe, can be a little bit tart. Greengages are incredibly sweet and perfect for adding to blended drinks, while damsons are fairly sour with a strong flavour, so are generally cooked with sugar before using. Prunes are dried plums and are intensely sweet – they can be blended with water for a thick sweet juice, and they combine well with most citrus fruits.

As with other sweet, soft fruit, plums are best used with other fruits that are less sweet or with more liquid ingredients, such as slightly sour apple juice. If plums are a little underripe, they will work well with extremely sweet fruits, such as bananas, mangoes or even orange juice.

Therapeutic uses Plums and prunes are known for their laxative properties. They are also very rich in potent antioxidants, making them a good choice for general health. Plums are a rich source of vitamin E and are good for maintaining healthy skin.

Quinces

These are an old-fashioned fruit but they are now becoming increasingly available throughout the year. Apple or pear-like in shape, depending on the variety, and with a pale golden colour, they have a delightful scented taste when cooked, but when eaten raw the flavour can be very astringent.

Quinces are hard when grown in cooler climates but ripen to a much softer texture when grown in warm climates. Although they are most often used in jellies and jams, for juicing purposes quinces should be prepared like apples, and are juiced in the same way. They should ideally be combined with sweet flavours, such as peach or apricot, to counteract their tart, slightly bitter taste.

Therapeutic uses Elixir of quince was traditionally used, many years ago, to help invalids through long periods of convalescence.

Below: If you find fresh quinces, prepare and juice them as you would apples, then combine with very sweet flavoured fruit juices and pulps such as mango or peach.

DRIED FRUIT

These are widely available and include raisins, sultanas (golden raisins) and currants, apricots, prunes, figs, mangoes, papaya, banana, apple rings and dates. Dried fruits do not juice well because they are dehydrated; however, they can be rehydrated by soaking in hot water, tea (Earl Grey is delicious), warmed wine or fortified wine. Adding cinnamon or another spice, such as cloves, complements their flavour. Dried fruits provide more concentrated sources of nutrients – including iron, magnesium and antioxidants – than their fresh equivalents. They are very sweet, so a little goes a long way in smoothies and blended drinks.

Above: Semi-dried apricots do not need soaking before use.

Above: Clockwise from top left, sultanas, currants and raisins can be finely chopped and added to smoothies or fruit blends.

Berries and currants

Tiny delicious currants and ripe berries are ideal for making smoothies and shakes. You will need a blender or a food processor for this because soft fruits do not go through juicers well. Berries are mainly a summer fruit and this is when they not only taste their best but are also cheapest, although they are often available at other times of the year when they are imported. They must be stored in the refrigerator and used within two days of purchase at most. Berries need careful handling and you need to watch them as they can quickly become overripe. If you cannot find fresh berries and currants, frozen ones are a good option.

Weight for weight, strawberries, raspberries and blackcurrants contain as much vitamin C as citrus fruits. Dark red berries are also rich sources of proanthocyanins, which are powerful antioxidants. Some people have an allergic reaction to strawberries and other berries, especially if they eat too many, and this can result in a strawberry rash or even a fever.

FREEZING FRUIT
If there is a glut of berries you can freeze them for blending at other times of the year.

Remove the stalks and leaves, then place the fruit on a baking sheet in a single layer to freeze. Once frozen transfer to a freezerproof container or bag. When you want to use them, either defrost first or blend from frozen for an iced effect.

Preparing and Blending Berries and Currants
To juice berries and currants, you will need either a blender or a food processor, a chopping board and a small, sharp knife.

Soft fruits These are easy to prepare for blending. Rinse, if you like, then discard any overripe or mouldy fruit. Remove any stems and leaves, either pulling them off by hand or using a sharp knife. Remove the calyx from strawberries, but remember there is no need to hull them when juicing.

To use a blender Place the prepared soft fruits in the flask, add liquid, such as water, fruit juice, milk or milk substitute, cover and select the appropriate speed. Add banana, other soft fruits, yogurt or cream to make a thicker consistency.

To use a food processor Place the prepared fruit in the bowl, cover and process. If you prefer a thinner consistency, the resulting pulp can be diluted by adding mineral water (still or sparkling, depending on your preference), a liquid juice such as orange juice, milk or a milk substitute.

Adding ice Create a delicious berry ice crush by adding plenty of ice to the blend. Before crushing ice in a blender of food processor, however, check the manufacturer's instructions.

MAKING A FRUIT COULIS
Coulis make delicious, jewel-coloured additions to trickle over a smoothie or milkshake, or even an ice cream, before serving.

1 Choose one fruit depending on the colour or flavour you want: raspberries or strawberries for dark red or pinkish red, peeled kiwi fruit for bright green or soaked dried apricots for a vibrant orange colour.

2 Put the fruit in a blender – approximately one small handful per person should be enough. Blend on high speed until puréed. If using dried apricots you will need to add 15–30ml/1–2 tbsp water before blending to achieve the correct consistency.

3 Strain the raspberry or strawberry coulis if you want a seedless purée.

When in season these fruits will be reasonably priced and can be used as a base for blends and smoothies, but at other times, when the fruit is more expensive, just a few berries will add a really distinctive taste and colour to drinks. They blend well with bananas, orange juice, apples, melons, peaches and most other delicately flavoured fruits. Blackberries will dominate the colour of most other juices, turning the blend a deep purple, but the taste is subtle enough to mix well with most fruit and vegetable combinations. Blackberries go particularly well with apples – a classic combination.

Therapeutic uses Strawberries are rich in pectin and ellagic acid, which makes them excellent for cleansing and detoxification. All four berries are good sources of proanthocyanins and have lots of vitamin C, both of which are good for boosting the immune system. As an antioxidant, vitamin C may even reduce the risk of developing certain cancers. Berries are a valuable source of calcium, which is important for healthy bones and teeth, and they are also soothing for the nervous system. People with cardiovascular health problems should include berries in their diet for their antioxidant properties. Raspberry juice is believed to cleanse the digestive system, and raspberries have traditionally been used in the treatment of diarrhoea, indigestion and rheumatism.

Above: Buy plenty of strawberries for juicing when they are in season.

Strawberries, Raspberries, Blackberries and Mulberries

Generally sweet but with a sharp undertone, strawberries are at their best and sweetest when perfectly ripe. Wild strawberries are much smaller than cultivated strawberries and have an intense, delicious flavour, but they are generally too expensive to blend unless you are lucky enough to have your own supply. Buy brightly coloured, plump berries and do not wash them until you are ready to use them.

Raspberries are a delicate berry so handle them with care, giving them just a light rinse, if necessary. They are more tart tasting than strawberries and they add a deeper reddish colour than the light pinky colour that strawberries give. Try a classic strawberry milkshake or a raspberry and peach smoothie to sample these fruits at their best.

Blackberries arrive later in the summer season than other berries, usually just as autumn is approaching. They grow wild in the countryside in abundance, but you can also find cultured blackberries in large supermarkets. They are very sweet and juicy when fully ripe.

Mulberries look a bit like blackberries in size and shape but they are less widely available. When ripe, their flavour is sweet but slightly sour and they are less aromatic than other berries.

Above: Raspberries add a delicious tart flavour and a vibrant red colour.

Right: Hunt for wild blackberry bushes, then pick your own.

Above: The intense colour of blueberries will dominate any blend you add them to.

Blueberries

Also called bilberries, blueberries are very sweet when ripe, but rather tart when underripe. Generally, they have a short summer season, though in warm countries the season is prolonged. Buy plenty and freeze them in small bags.

As with blackberries, the dark juice of blueberries will dominate the blend; in this case the juice is a rich bluish-purple. They are a delicious addition to most fruit blends, if you prefer you could just add sparkling mineral water to a thick blueberry purée.

Therapeutic uses Blueberries are one of the most potent fruits in terms of antioxidant power. Primarily used to boost the immune system, they also play an important role in eye health. During World War II, pilots ate blueberries because they believed it would improve their night vision. As with cranberries, they are good for relieving urinary tract infections.

Blackcurrants, Redcurrants and Whitecurrants

The general flavour of blackcurrants is sour-sweet, depending on how ripe they are. They are best sweetened, although this is not necessary if you are mixing a small amount of blackcurrant juice with a sweeter fruit. They make ideal mixers but they are not good juiced on their own. Blackcurrants are more often made into cordials than into juices, and you could add some cordial to a blend made of other fruits.

Redcurrants and whitecurrants are available at the same time of the year as blackcurrants but are less abundant and can be more difficult to find. They are good mixed with less expensive blackcurrants in blends and smoothies.

Therapeutic uses Few fruits and vegetables have more vitamin C than blackcurrants, making them powerful allies in wintertime for fending off colds and flu. Blackcurrant pips (seeds) are a rich source of essential fatty acids (the same as those in evening primrose oil), which are helpful for female hormonal health, relieving symptoms of pre-menstrual syndrome and mastalgia (sore breasts).

Left: Whitecurrants are sweeter than other currants and less tart.

Left: Mix redcurrants with sweeter ingredients for a delicious blend.

Above: Tart blackcurrants contain more vitamin C than almost any other fruit, but are best used in small quantities.

*Above:
Cranberries mix
well with sweet orchard
fruits, such as pear.*

The berry is too tiny and sour for juicing, but makes an excellent sweet syrup when boiled with sugar and water. Elderflower syrup is a traditional immune-boosting remedy. In spring and early summer, the flowers are gathered and can be used to make delicious and fragrant elderflower cordial.

Cranberries

These lovely berries are associated with the winter season as they are generally not available fresh at other times of the year. Buy them when available and keep them in your freezer until needed. Cranberries are fairly sour and need to be sweetened. They can work exceptionally well with other fruit such as sweet oranges, apples, pears or carrots, choose your combination for a delicious, summery smoothie.

Therapeutic uses Cranberries are very successful at preventing or resolving cystitis and other urinary tract infections when drunk as a juice over several days. The antioxidants they contain specifically target the bacteria of the urinary tract and prevent them from adhering and causing damage. The quinine contained in cranberries is an effective liver detoxifier.

Other Berries

Elderberries These are not generally available in the shops but must be gathered from the wild. The elder tree grows widely and can be found in many urban gardens. It is not uncommon for people to disregard it as a weed.

Gooseberries These have a short summer season but can be frozen on baking sheets. They are widely available but not often used for making drinks because they can be extremely sour. However, you could add a small number to a blend to gain the benefit of their immune-supporting effects.

Below: Raw, elderberries can be boiled with sugar to make a syrup.

*Left: Freeze
gooseberries to
use all year
round.*

Exotic and other fruits

Most exotic fruits are now available year round. These fruits are mainly blended because, apart from melons and pineapples, they will not go through a juicer very well. Melons, pineapples and bananas produce enough juice to use as base ingredients, but the availability and yield of other exotic fruits mean that they are best used in smaller quantities. Orange-coloured fruits, such as mangoes, are excellent sources of betacarotene.

Preparing and Juicing Exotic and Other Fruits

You will need a blender or food processor, a juicer (centrifugal or masticating), a chopping board and a sharp knife. A spoon is useful for scooping the flesh out of some fruits.

Melons Cut a wedge and scoop out the pips (seeds). Cut away the flesh and purée in a blender or food processor. Firmer melons can be put through a juicer, particularly watermelon.

Bananas Peel and then break the flesh into chunks. Put the banana into a blender or food processor and blend to a pulp, then add other fruit juice until you get the right consistency.

Pineapples Lie the pineapple on its side on a chopping board, then, using a large sharp knife, slice off the base and the top. Cut the fruit into thick slices, then remove the skin. The flesh can be put in a blender or food processor, or pushed through a juicer.

Kiwi fruit, papaya and guava Cut the fruit in half. For papaya and guava, scoop out the seeds. For all three fruits, either scoop out the ripe flesh with a spoon or peel with a sharp knife. Put the flesh in a blender or food processor. None of these yields enough juice when put through a juicer.

Mangoes Slice down either side of the stone. Score the flesh into small squares, then push the skin from the outside and cut off the flesh into a blender or food processor.

Lychees The easiest way to peel lychees is by hand; the skin is slightly stiff and cracks easily. Ease the fruit out and remove the stone. Put the flesh in a blender or food processor. Lychees do not yield enough juice in a juicer.

RHUBARB

Traces of oxalic acid, which inhibits calcium and iron absorption and may exacerbate joint problems, can be found in many vegetables. The high levels of oxalic acid in rhubarb mean that it should not be used raw, and rhubarb leaves should never be eaten because they are poisonous. Rhubarb can, however, be added to drinks if it is cooked first. It contains high levels of calcium, potassium and thiamine (vitamin B_1).

Right: Add bananas to smoothies for a thick, creamy taste.

The enzymes also help to clear the blood and break down clots. Pineapple is thought to relieve arthritis and may help to reduce back pain. This fruit also helps to get rid of mucus build-up.

Kiwi Fruit

Like the banana, kiwi fruit was once exotic but is now very easy to buy. If kiwi fruit are hard when bought they will ripen quickly on a windowsill. They taste sweet, zesty and aromatic when ripe and are inexpensive enough to use as a base juice. They combine well with other green fruits, such as apples or grapes, as well as tropical fruits.

Therapeutic uses Kiwi fruit is one of the richest sources of immune-boosting and collagen-building vitamin C.

Above: Kiwi fruit make a delicious, tangy base juice.

Bananas

Once an exotic fruit, bananas are now a staple. Smaller and much more flavourful bananas are becoming generally available and they are well worth buying.

Bananas provide an excellent base for a smoothie and combine well with many different fruits, although they are not good when partnered with vegetables. They are a great way to thicken a blend and make it more filling, especially if you don't want to use dairy products.

Therapeutic uses Bananas are very good energy boosters and they are full of bowel-supporting, gentle fibre.

Therapeutic uses Fresh pineapples contain one of the strongest protein-digesting enzymes, bromelain, making them valuable for all digestive complaints. They even "tidy up" the digestive tract by skimming off dead cells, and they can help to heal damaged digestive tracts.

Pineapples

These are sweet to sweet-sharp tasting, often with an aromatic note. Pineapples do not ripen further once harvested, so make sure you buy a fruit that is ripe. Select a pineapple that is slightly soft to the touch, smells delicious and has a good colour with no green patches. The leaves should be crisp and green, with no sign of yellowing at the tips. Pineapple combines extremely well with most fruits and also with vegetable juices.

Above: Pineapples can be mixed with most fruits.

Left: Ripe mangoes have extremely soft flesh that is juicy and sweet.

Above: Aromatic lychees contain significant amounts of vitamin C.

Mangoes, Papayas and Guavas

These fruits are best bought ripe, when they yield slightly to gentle pressure, which is when they are at their sweetest. They are all aromatic, delicious and luxurious tasting. They combine well with banana and orange juice, apples or carrot to make tasty tropical smoothies.

Therapeutic uses Papaya is distinguished by its potent digestive enzyme, papain, which has all the advantages of bromelain (see pineapples). Papain also has a reputation for helping to restore healthy bowel flora (bacterial balance). All three fruits are rich in betacarotene and contain generous amounts of vitamin C as well as many minerals, making them excellent all-round sources of nutrition.

Lychees

These have a subtle, aromatic and sweet taste. They need to be combined with equally delicately flavoured fruits so that their flavour is not lost. Combine them in smoothie blends with melons, bananas, apples or strawberries.

Therapeutic uses Lychees are a good source of vitamin C.

Right: The juice of Galia melons is delicious when combined with either fruit or vegetables.

Melons

There are many different types of melon available, including cantaloupe, honeydew and watermelon. They are members of the gourd family, which also includes cucumbers and squashes. To choose a ripe melon (apart from watermelon), press the blossom end, which should yield slightly to gentle pressure. A ripe melon will have a sweet, perfumed aroma. For watermelon, tap the side of the fruit, which should sound hollow; the rind should barely give when pressed with a thumb.

Melons make a sweet, refreshing base for a blend that combines well with other fruits, such as tart apples or pears, or with bitter vegetables such as cabbage.

Therapeutic uses Melons have a diuretic and digestive cleansing action, and they are good for all problem skin conditions. The pips (seeds) are very rich in potassium, which helps to lower high blood pressure, and they are also valued for their zinc and vitamin E content, so it is worthwhile including a few. All of the orange-fleshed melons are rich in betacarotene, which is good for the immune system and for eye health in general. Watermelon also provides the phytonutrient lycopene, which is reputedly powerful in fighting against certain types of cancer, including prostate cancer. Lycopene must be consumed together with a small amount of fat to facilitate absorption, and supplements are recommended to gain its full benefit.

Grapes

Depending on the variety, grapes can be sweet or tart tasting. Black, red, green (or white) grapes are available, and you can choose from seeded or seedless varieties. They produce a light green or pink juice depending on the colour of the grape.

Grapes are fairly watery so they work well with fruits that produce thicker juice, such as mangoes, papayas, peaches or plums. They are a useful and delicious addition to most fruit and vegetable blends.

Therapeutic uses Dark-skinned grapes are rich in a compound called resveratrol, one of the most potent antioxidants, as well as proanthocyanins, and all colours of grapes have high levels of ellagic acid, which is a potent detoxifier. Grape juice is a traditional naturopathic rest cure and is also sometimes used as a nerve tonic. Grapes have been reported to help alleviate the symptoms of arthritis.

Right: There is no need to remove grape pips before blending as they will just be incorporated into the juice.

TROPICAL TOPPERS
Some tropical fruits are not good for juicing as they either yield too little juice or are too fiddly to prepare. Try using them as pretty decorations and toppings.

Figs Cut from the pointed end downwards but do not cut right through the base. Make a second cut at right angles to the first, creating a cross shape. Squeeze the fruit gently to open up into a "flower". This makes an attractive edible decoration – eat them with the skin on. Figs do not yield much juice but you can combine them with other juices. They have a strong laxative action, so should be consumed in moderation, and are useful for irritated bronchial tubes.

Star fruit (carambola) These pretty tropical fruits can be sliced very thinly into attractive star-shaped decorations.

Pomegranates Cut these in half and scoop out the scarlet pips (seeds), separating them from the pith. Sweet, refreshing and crunchy, the pips are ideal for sprinkling on top of juices and smoothies.

Passion fruit Cut in half and scoop out the pulp and pips (seeds). Sweet, aromatic and attractive, this pulp makes an ideal juice topping.

Dates Cut dates in half and discard the stone (pit). Although they cannot be juiced, they can be chopped and added to blends. Otherwise, slice thinly and serve as a side snack with a drink.

Dairy and dairy alternatives

Adding milk, yogurts, dairy or milk substitutes to blended drinks results in a more luxurious and creamy, though not necessarily more fattening, treat. Milk is calcium-rich (even skimmed milk) and many alternative milks are also now enriched with calcium. You can keep a lid on calorie and fat counts by choosing low-fat versions. Dairy substitutes are useful for people with dairy intolerances, meaning they can still add creamy texture to smoothies and milkshakes.

Milk

For a rich and creamy taste choose full cream (whole) milk. Most people, however, need to avoid too much saturated fat in their diet and would be better advised to use skimmed or semi-skimmed (low-fat) milk.

Therapeutic uses Milk is one of the richest sources of calcium available. Full cream milk is only usually advised for young children, who need the calories it provides to promote growth and bone health.

Below: Yogurt is available in many forms, both low-fat and full-fat. Natural yogurt is ideal, but you could experiment with low-fat flavoured yogurts.

Cream

For extra indulgence, use double (heavy) or single (light) cream, crème fraîche, mascarpone, smetana or, for a different taste, sour cream.

Therapeutic uses Cream is an excellent source of vitamin E, which helps to maintain healthy skin, but it is very high in calories so should be used in moderation.

Yogurt

For making shakes or smoothies thicker, yogurts are an extremely useful ingredient. Greek (US strained plain) yogurt is much thicker than standard varieties but has almost as many calories as cream, so it should not be used on a regular basis. Low-fat yogurts, including low-fat Greek yogurt, are readily available instead, so you can still indulge yourself without feeling too guilty. Fruit yogurts can add interesting flavours to fruity blends.

Therapeutic uses Yogurt is rich in calcium and it is often suitable even for people who have a milk intolerance. Choosing live "bio" yogurt can help improve digestive tract health by providing healthy bacteria. High-fibre yogurts that have cholesterol-lowering properties are now available.

Above: Many low-fat alternative milks are now calcium-enriched.

ALTERNATIVE MILKS

Often used by people who have a dairy allergy, alternative milks are a good low-calorie option. The fats in most nut milks, except for coconut, are healthy polyunsaturated fats.

Soya milk Choose the calcium-enriched variety of soya milk if you are using it instead of cow's milk on a regular basis.
Rice milk This has a thinner and lighter consistency than cow's milk, but a deliciously sweet flavour. Vanilla- and chocolate-flavoured rice milks are also available.
Oat milk This alternative to cow's milk is extremely rich and has a creamy, smooth taste.
Nut milks Coconut milk is delicious but, because it has a very rich flavour, it is best if you either dilute it or use just a small amount. You can now buy almond milk and various other nut milks from most large supermarkets or health food shops.

Above: Use real strawberry ice cream to make a traditional milkshake.

Frozen Ingredients

Ice creams, sorbets (sherbets), frozen yogurts and soya ices can all be scooped straight from the freezer to make a delicious old-fashioned shake.
Therapeutic uses Dairy ice cream is a good source of calcium, although it is high in calories, but non-dairy ice creams and sorbets do not have the benefit of calcium.

Low-fat Creamy Ingredients

Fromage frais (cream cheese) and plain cottage cheese can both be bought in low-fat versions and used as creamy thickeners, as can buttermilk which is slightly sour tasting.
Therapeutic uses These are perfect for anybody on a calorie-controlled diet.

Tofu

Also known as soya bean curd and beancurd, tofu is available in three different textures: firm, medium-firm and silken. Naturally a fairly bland food with a slight nutty taste, it will affect the texture of drinks, but not the taste. Soft, silken tofu has the best texture for blending and adds a creamy thickness to the blend.
Therapeutic uses Tofu is an all-round healthy food – high in protein, low in saturated fats and calories, easy to digest and cholesterol-free. It has high levels of calcium and lots of vitamin E, which is important for maintaining healthy skin and helps protect against heart disease.

Below: Tofu is rich in hormone-balancing phytoestrogens, which can help protect against some cancers.

EGGS

Raw eggs contain high levels of vitamin B12, which is vital for the nervous system. Eggs are often used as the basis of protein shakes by sports enthusiasts or in hangover remedies to kick-start the system. Before using raw eggs in a blend, you should be aware of the following:

• Raw egg white binds with the B-vitamin biotin and, if overused, can lead to a deficiency of this nutrient.
• Pregnant women, children, the sick or elderly, or those with an impaired immune system should not consume raw eggs, because of the risk of salmonella. (While chickens are often routinely vaccinated for salmonella in some countries, there is still a residual risk from unvaccinated flocks.)
• Eggs have a high cholesterol content, contained in the yolk. People who have high cholesterol levels may benefit from limiting their egg intake to five a week. However, as we make most of the cholesterol in the body (cholesterol is needed for cell maintenance) and this is adversely affected by a high saturated fat intake, it is more beneficial to reduce saturated fats from butter, cheese and meat.
• Eggs that have been produced to contain high levels of omega-3 fatty acids are now widely available and these could make an important contribution to heart health.

Above: Raw eggs can thicken blends nicely but it is not safe for everybody to eat them.

Sweeteners and other flavourings

We are all naturally attracted to sweet-tasting foods. The advantage of blended drinks and smoothies is that it is possible to give in to that craving occasionally, with some indulgent additions, and yet still know that you are benefiting from the healthy basic ingredients.

Many juices, pulps and blends, whether made from fruit or vegetables, are naturally sweet, so you may find that you need to dilute them to reduce their sweetness. This can be done by adding one-third to one-half water – either still or sparkling, according to taste. You could also add a milky ingredients. Adding water or milk will ensure that blood sugar levels rise more slowly. Children should always drink fruit juices that are diluted to reduce the impact on their teeth.

If a blend, smoothie or milkshake is not sweet enough, you could add sugar – white, brown or muscovado (molasses) – or flavoured syrups, such as vanilla, or fruit cordials. There are, however, many other sweeteners that can be used.

Honey

Different honeys have varying tastes, depending on which type of pollen the bees have gathered. Popular choices are lavender or apple blossom honey, which have a fragrant sweetness. Manuka honey is renowned for its health-promoting properties; it is anti-bacterial, making it ideal for sore throats. Honey should not be fed to children under the age of 12 months as it could cause botulism, a type of food poisoning that can be fatal.

Fructose

Instead of using table sugar (sucrose) you could use fructose (a totally natural fruit sugar). This has a lower Glycaemic Index (GI) score than sucrose so can be used in moderation by diabetics. (The GI is a measure of how fast a carbohydrate enters the blood stream as sugar. The higher the score, the less healthy the carbohydrate.) Fructose is sweeter than table sugar so do not use as a direct substitution in drinks.

Blackstrap Molasses

During the refining of sugar, the juice squeezed from the cane or beet is boiled until syrupy and then the sugar crystals are extracted. There are three boilings, resulting in light molasses, then dark and finally blackstrap molasses, which is thick, dark and rather bitter. It is a rich source of calcium, iron and magnesium but only a little should be used.

Above: Blackstrap molasses is intensely sweet and so only a tiny bit is needed.

Above: Choose from many different flavours and types of honey.

Above: Liven up parties by adding a few shots of alcohol to your punchbowl.

Above: Try crumbling brownies on top of your favourite chocolate milkshake.

Above: When added to your blends, meringues give an irresistible crunch.

FOS (fructo-oligosaccharide)

This is a natural fibre found in bananas, Jerusalem artichokes, tomatoes, onions and many other fruits and vegetables. It looks like sugar and is almost as sweet but it has no effect on blood sugar levels. It can be found in health food shops. Using a moderate amount has a beneficial effect on digestive tract health as it promotes the growth of good bacteria, but too much FOS can lead to bloating.

Other Flavourings

Many other ingredients and sweet additions can be included in smoothies. Health-promoting properties become less important here – everyone deserves to indulge themselves occasionally.

Coffee Freshly ground or instant, coffee is just the thing if you need a wake-up call with your morning blend. Try adding it to creamy blends to make a coffee-flavoured smoothie or shake. Use decaffeinated coffee if you are caffeine sensitive and, if you are feeling particularly virtuous, try using dandelion coffee, which is reputed to have liver-cleansing properties.

Chocolate This is an irresistible ingredient, whether melted, grated or in powder form. Dark (bittersweet) chocolate is the best for you as it is rich in iron and antioxidants, but for a milder flavour you should use milk chocolate. For a decadent finish, grate or shave chocolate on top of your smoothie – dark, plain (semisweet), milk or white, whichever you prefer.

Sweets (candies) Try adding sweets to the side of the glass as a decoration that is guaranteed to impress at a kid's party, or add them to the blender and blend them into the drink. Turkish delight or nougat are good choices, or you could serve a smoothie with an edible swizzle stick in the shape of a chocolate wand.

Cakes and cookies Brownies or meringues can be crumbled on top of smoothies or added to the blend for texture, and any other cakes or cookies can be used instead if they complement the drink you are serving. Amaretti provide a lovely almond accent, for example, which would be delicious with strawberry, apricot or peach-based blends, or try crunchy coconut macaroons sprinkled on top of a tropical fruit blend.

Alcohol Add a splash of alcohol to your favourite drinks when you just want to relax with a smoothie at the end of the day, or give your party juices a boost. Choose different drinks for their flavours, such as coffee, mint or orange liqueurs, or give your blend a real kick by adding a shot (or two) of brandy or whisky.

Above: Create a traditional, decadent milkshake with rich, dark chocolate.

easy breakfast blends

Breakfast is the most important meal of the day but also the most neglected, so give yourself a kick-start with these fuel-packed, imaginative drinks. Made in minutes and easier to digest than a bowl of cereal, fabulous fresh fruit blends and decadent smoothies provide the perfect early-morning boost.

Creamy banana boost

Bananas are a great energy food. They are packed with valuable nutrients and healthy carbohydrates, and they also fill you up – which is definitely a bonus. Blended with the additional fruits – pineapple, dates and lemon juice – and creamy milk, this delicious concoction will keep you going for hours. If you're prone to snacking throughout the day, try this and you'll feel all the better for it. Any leftover drink can be stored in the refrigerator for up to a day.

Makes 2–3 tall glasses

½ pineapple
4 Medjool dates, pitted
1 small ripe banana
juice of 1 lemon
300ml/½ pint/1¼ cups very cold full cream (whole) milk or soya milk

Cook's tip
The Medjool date is considered to be the jewel of all dates because of its size, texture and sweetness. It originates from Morocco, where it was reserved for royal hosts and other dignitaries centuries ago. Nowadays we can all enjoy them.

1 Using a small, sharp knife, cut away the skin and core from the pineapple. Roughly chop the flesh and put it in a blender or food processor, then add the pitted dates.

2 Peel and chop the banana and add it to the rest of the fruit together with the lemon juice.

3 Blend thoroughly until smooth, stopping to scrape the mixture down from the side of the bowl with a rubber spatula, if necessary.

4 Add the milk to the blender or food processor and process briefly until well combined. Pour the smoothie into tall glasses and serve immediately.

Zesty soya smoothie

Whizzed up with freshly squeezed orange juice, a splash of tangy lemon and a little fragrant honey, tofu can be transformed into a drink that's smooth, creamy, nutritious and delicious. Most people would not think to add tofu to a blended drink, but please do try it – you will be genuinely surprised. If possible, try to get hold of some silken tofu for this smoothie, as it has a wonderful satiny texture that blends particularly well.

Makes 1 large glass

2 oranges
15ml/1 tbsp lemon juice
20–25ml/4–5 tsp sunflower honey or herb honey
150g/5oz tofu
long, thin strips of pared orange rind, to decorate

Cook's tip
If you prefer a smooth drink, strain the liquid through a sieve after blending to remove the orange rind.

1 Finely grate the rind of one orange and set aside. Use a citrus juicer to juice both oranges and pour the juice into a food processor or blender. Add the grated orange rind, lemon juice, sunflower or herb honey and tofu.

2 Whizz the ingredients until smooth and creamy, then pour into a glass. Decorate with the pared orange rind and serve.

Opposite: Creamy banana boost (left) and Zesty soya smoothie (right)

Dairy-free deluxe

Prunes, apples, oranges and soya milk may seem like an unusual combination but the results are absolutely fabulous. Sweet, caramel-rich and very drinkable, this is a great milkshake for both adults and children, and, of course, for anyone on a dairy-free diet. Regular cow's milk can be used, if you prefer, but if you are watching the calories, use skimmed milk. The resulting drink will not be quite as creamy, but it will still be delicious.

Makes 1 tall glass

2 small eating apples
5 ready-to-eat pitted prunes
juice of 1 orange
60ml/4 tbsp soya milk
ice cubes

Cook's tip
Any eating apples can be used for this drink. If you prefer a tart flavour opt for a Granny Smith or a Cox's Pippin; if not, go for a sweet apple like the Royal Gala.

1 Using a small, sharp knife, remove the core from the apples and chop into chunks – but do not peel them. Push half the chopped apple through a juicer, followed by the prunes and the remaining chopped apple.

2 Pour the apple and prune juice into a jug (pitcher) and add the orange juice and soya milk. Whisk lightly until smooth and frothy. Pour into a chunky glass and serve immediately, adding a few cubes of ice.

Pear flair

For a truly refreshing combination, you can't do much better than a mixture of juicy pears and grapes. Wheatgerm adds body for a sustained energy fix and soya yogurt turns the juice into a protein-packed milkshake with a lusciously light and frothy topping. This really is quite a filling drink and is a great choice for those who feel that their life is too busy to prepare really nutritious food. A quick and easy drink that is good for you too – what could be better?

Makes 1 large glass

1 large pear
150g/5oz/1¼ cups green grapes
15ml/1 tbsp wheatgerm
60ml/4 tbsp soya yogurt
ice cubes

Cook's tip
If you would prefer to use a dairy yogurt rather than the soya variety, substitute with the type of your choice. It is better that you stick with a natural (plain) yogurt as plenty of fruity flavour is gained from the pear and the grapes. Look for the 0 per cent fat varieties.

1 Using a vegetable peeler, peel the pear and chop the flesh into large chunks of roughly the same size.

2 Push half the pear chunks through a juicer, followed by the grapes and then the remaining chunks of pear. Transfer the juice to a small jug (pitcher).

3 Add the wheatgerm to the yogurt and stir to mix throughly.

4 Pour into the pear and grape juice, whisking until it is light and frothy. Pour the milkshake over ice cubes and serve.

Opposite: Dairy-free deluxe (left) and Pear flair (right)

Orange and raspberry smoothie

This exquisite blend combines the sharp-sweet taste of raspberries and the refreshing fruitiness of oranges with smooth yogurt. It tastes like creamy, fruit heaven in a glass. Even better, it takes just minutes to prepare, making it perfect as a quick breakfast juice for people in a hurry or, indeed, as a refreshing drink at any other time of day.

1 Place the raspberries and yogurt in a blender or food processor and process for about 1 minute until the mixture is smooth and creamy.

2 Add the orange juice to the raspberry and yogurt mixture and process for another 30 seconds or until thoroughly combined. Pour into tall glasses and serve immediately.

Makes 2–3 glasses

250g/9oz/1⅓ cups raspberries, chilled
200ml/7fl oz/scant 1 cup natural (plain) yogurt, chilled
300ml/½ pint/1¼ cups freshly squeezed orange juice, chilled

Cook's tip
For a super-chilled version, use frozen raspberries instead of fresh. You may need to blend the raspberries and yogurt for a little longer to get a really smooth result.

Mango and lime lassi

Inspired by the classic Indian drink, this tangy, fruity blend is great for breakfast or as a delicious pick-me-up at any time of day. Soft, ripe mango blended with yogurt and sharp, zesty lime and lemon juice makes a wonderfully thick, cooling drink that's packed with energy. It can also be enjoyed as a mellow soother when you need to unwind.

Makes 2 tall glasses

1 mango
finely grated rind and juice of 1 lime
15ml/1 tbsp lemon juice
5–10ml/1–2 tsp caster (superfine) sugar
100ml/3½fl oz/scant ½ cup natural
   (plain) yogurt
mineral water
1 extra lime, halved, to serve

1 Peel the mango and cut the flesh from the stone (pit). Put the flesh into a blender or food processor and add the lime rind and juice.

2 Add the lemon juice, sugar and natural yogurt. Whizz until completely smooth, scraping down the sides of the bowl, if necessary. Stir in a little mineral water to thin it down.

3 Serve immediately, with half a lime on the side of each glass so that more juice can be squeezed in, if desired.

Sweet dream

A soothing blend guaranteed to wake you up slowly, this fruity threesome is naturally sweet so there is no need for any additional sugar. Fresh grapefruit juice marries brilliantly with the dried fruits, and rich creamy yogurt makes a delicious contrast of colour and flavour – simply perfect to sip over a leisurely breakfast while reading the newspaper.

Makes 2 glasses

25g/1oz/scant ¼ cup dried figs or
  dates, stoned (pitted)
50g/2oz/¼ cup ready-to-eat prunes
25g/1oz/scant ¼ cup sultanas (golden raisins)
1 grapefruit
350ml/12fl oz/1½ cups full cream
  (whole) milk
30ml/2 tbsp Greek (US strained plain) yogurt

Cook's tip
For a dairy-free version of this drink, omit the yogurt and use soya or rice milk instead of ordinary milk. The consistency of the smoothie will not be as creamy but it will still be delicious – and perhaps better for those who prefer a lighter drink.

1 Put the dried fruits in a blender or food processor. Squeeze the grapefruit juice and add to the machine. Blend until smooth, scraping the mixture down from the side of the bowl, if necessary. Add the milk and blend until completely smooth.

2 Using a teaspoon, tap a spoonful of the yogurt around the inside of each of two tall glasses. Pour in the fruit mixture and serve immediately.

Raspberry and oatmeal smoothie

Just a spoonful or so of oatmeal gives substance to this tangy, invigorating drink. If you can, prepare it ahead of time because soaking the raw oats helps to break down the starch into natural sugars that are easy to digest. The smoothie will thicken up in the refrigerator so you might need to stir in a little extra juice or mineral water just before serving.

Makes 1 large glass

25ml/1½ tbsp medium oatmeal
150g/5oz/scant 1 cup raspberries
5–10ml/1–2 tsp clear honey
45ml/3 tbsp natural (plain) yogurt

1 Spoon the oatmeal into a heatproof bowl. Pour in 120ml/4fl oz/½ cup boiling water and leave to stand for about 10 minutes.

2 Put the soaked oats in a blender or food processor and add all but two or three of the raspberries, the honey and about 30ml/2 tbsp of the yogurt. Process until smooth, scraping down the side of the bowl if necessary.

Cook's tip

If you don't like raspberry pips (seeds) in your smoothies, press the fruit through a sieve with the back of a wooden spoon to make a smooth purée, then process with the oatmeal and yogurt as before. Alternatively, try using redcurrants instead of the raspberries.

Although a steaming bowl of porridge can't be beaten as a winter warmer, this smooth, oaty drink makes a great, light alternative in warmer months. It is a good way to make sure you get your fill of wholesome oats for breakfast.

3 Pour the raspberry and oatmeal smoothie into a large glass, swirl in the remaining yogurt and top with the reserved raspberries.

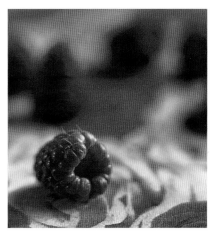

Big breakfast

Easy to prepare and even easier to drink, this energy-packed smoothie makes a great start to the day. Bananas and sesame seeds provide the perfect fuel in the form of slow-release carbohydrate that will keep you going all morning, while fresh and zesty orange juice and sweet, scented mango will set your tastebuds tingling first thing.

Makes 2 glasses

½ mango
1 banana
1 large orange
30ml/2 tbsp wheat bran
15ml/1 tbsp sesame seeds
10–15ml/2–3 tsp honey

Cook's tip
Mango juice is naturally very sweet so you may wish to add less honey or leave it out altogether. Taste the drink to decide how much you need.

1 Using a small, sharp knife, skin the mango, then slice the flesh off the stone (pit). Peel the banana and break it into short lengths, then place it in a blender or food processor with the mango.

2 Squeeze the juice from the orange and add to the blender or food processor along with the bran, sesame seeds and honey. Whizz until the mixture is smooth and creamy, then pour into glasses and serve.

Muesli smoothly

Another great breakfast booster, this store-cupboard smoothie can be a lifesaver if you've run out of fresh fruit. It's also a perfect option for breakfast in bed without the crumbs. Any extra drink can be covered and stored overnight in the refrigerator, although you'll probably need to add more milk in the morning as it will undoubtedly thicken on standing.

Makes 2 glasses

1 piece preserved stem ginger, plus
    30ml/2 tbsp syrup from the ginger jar
50g/2oz/¼ cup ready-to-eat dried apricots,
    halved or quartered
40g/1½oz/scant ½ cup natural
    muesli (granola)
about 200ml/7fl oz/scant 1 cup
    semi-skimmed (low-fat) milk

Cook's tip
Apricot and ginger are perfect partners in this divine drink. It makes an incredibly healthy, tasty breakfast, but is so delicious and indulgent that you could even serve it as a dessert after a summer meal.

1 Chop the preserved ginger and put it in a blender or food processor with the syrup, apricots, muesli and milk.

2 Process until smooth, adding more milk if necessary. Serve in wide glasses.

Late breakfast

This energizing blend is simply bursting with goodness, just what you need when the morning has got off to a slow start. Not only is tofu a perfect source of protein, it is also rich in minerals and contains nutrients that protect against dangerous diseases. Blended with seeds and vitamin-rich strawberries, this creamy blend should see you through until lunchtime. Store any leftovers in the refrigerator for later in the day or the following morning.

Makes 2 glasses

250g/9oz firm tofu
200g/7oz/1¾ cups strawberries
45ml/3 tbsp pumpkin or sunflower seeds,
   plus extra for sprinkling
30–45ml/2–3 tbsp clear honey
juice of 2 large oranges
juice of 1 lemon

Cook's tip
Almost any other fruit can be used instead of the strawberries. Those that blend well, such as mangoes, bananas, peaches, plums and raspberries, work particularly well as a substitute.

1 Roughly chop the tofu, then hull and roughly chop the strawberries. Reserve a few strawberry chunks.

2 Put all the ingredients in a blender or food processor and blend until completely smooth, scraping the mixture down from the side of the bowl, if necessary.

3 Pour into tumblers and sprinkle with extra seeds and strawberry chunks.

A good fix

While some people thrive on a glass of freshly juiced fruits first thing in the morning, others can't quite get going without their daily caffeine fix in the form of strong coffee. This gorgeous mocha smoothie combines decadent dark chocolate and caffeine-rich coffee in a deliciously frothy energizing mix. This is an intensely sweet and indulgent way to start the day – so don't treat yourself too often.

Makes 1 large glass

40g/1½oz plain (semisweet) chocolate, plus extra for decoration
5–10ml/1–2 tsp instant espresso powder
300ml/½ pint/1¼ cups full cream (whole) milk
30ml/2 tbsp double (heavy) cream (optional)
ice cubes
cocoa powder (unsweetened), for dusting

1 Chop the chocolate into pieces and place in a small, heavy pan with the espresso powder and 100ml/3½fl oz/ scant ½ cup of the milk. Heat very gently, stirring with a wooden spoon, until the chocolate has melted. Remove from the heat and pour into a bowl. Leave to cool for 10 minutes.

2 Add the remaining milk and cream, if using, and whisk the mixture together until smooth and frothy – you could use a handheld blender wand. Pour the smoothie over ice cubes in a large glass or mug and serve sprinkled with cocoa powder and chocolate shavings.

smooth
and
simple

Refreshingly tangy or as smooth as silk, super

smoothies have earned their place as one of our

favourite drinks. Keep them simple with pure fruit

blends, or try something a little different by adding

creamed coconut, fruit tea, herbs or spices.

Let the ideas in this irresistible chapter inspire you

to experiment with all kinds of combinations.

Ruby dreamer

Figs have a distinctive yet delicate taste and are best used in simple combinations, with ingredients that enhance, rather than mask, their flavour. Like most fruits, fresh figs are now available most of the year round but they are often at their best in winter when ruby oranges are also in season – giving you the perfect excuse to make this veritable treat of a smoothie.

1 Cut off the hard, woody tips from the stalks of the figs, then use a sharp knife to cut each fruit in half.

2 Squeeze the oranges, using a citrus juicer or by hand. Pour the juice into a blender or food processor and add the figs and sugar. Process well until the mixture is really smooth and fairly thick, scraping the fruit down from the side of the bowl, if necessary.

3 Add lemon juice and blend briefly. Pour over crushed ice and serve.

Makes 2 glasses

6 large ripe figs
4 ruby oranges
15ml/1 tbsp dark muscovado (molasses) sugar
30–45ml/2–3 tbsp lemon juice
crushed ice

Cook's tip
If you cannot find ruby oranges, use any other type of orange. The colour of the juice, however, will not be quite so vibrant.

Mango mania

Even people on a dairy-free diet can enjoy rich, creamy, indulgent drinks. This one is made using soya milk, which is particularly good in milkshakes and smoothies. It has a lovely caramel flavour that blends brilliantly with fruit purées, especially those made from fruits with an intense, naturally sweet taste like mangoes.

Makes 2 tall glasses

1 medium mango
300ml/½ pint/1¼ cups soya milk
finely grated rind and juice of 1 lime,
    plus extra rind for garnish
15–30ml/1–2 tbsp clear honey
crushed ice

Cook's tip
If you like very sweet drinks, choose soya milk sweetened with apple juice for this recipe. It is readily available in supermarkets and has a really rich flavour.

1 Using a sharp knife, peel the mango and cut the flesh off the stone (pit). Place the chopped flesh in a blender or food processor and add the soya milk, lime rind and juice and a little honey. Blend until smooth and frothy.

2 Taste the mixture and add more honey, if you like, blending until well mixed. Place some crushed ice in two glasses, then pour over the smoothie. Sprinkle with lime rind and serve.

Smooth and simple

Pre-packed and ready to use, a mixed bag of summer fruits (which can be bought from the freezer section in most large supermarkets) makes an unbelievably simple, fruity base for drinks. The frozen fruits mean that the final blend is perfectly chilled as well, so you don't need to add ice. Mixed with orange juice and enriched with a tempting swirl of cream, this smoothie is made in a flash – the perfect accompaniment to a relaxing afternoon in the sunshine.

Makes 3 glasses

500g/1lb 2oz frozen mixed summer fruits, partially thawed
30ml/2 tbsp caster (superfine) sugar
about 300ml/½ pint/1¼ cups freshly squeezed orange juice
60ml/4 tbsp single (light) cream

Cook's tip
If you do not want to squeeze the oranges, you can buy juice – but avoid the concentrated types.

1 Tip all but a few of the summer fruits into a blender or food processor and add the sugar and orange juice. Blend until smooth, adding a little more orange juice if the mixture is too thick.

2 Pour the smoothie into 3 tall glasses and, using a teaspoon, swirl a little cream into each glass. Top with the reserved fruits and serve with long spoons to mix in the cream.

Fruit-tea smoothie

Depending on your preference you can use any of the varied assortment of fruit teas, now readily available in most large supermarkets, for this thick, creamy blend. This recipe uses dried apricots and apples but you could easily replace these with dried pears, peaches or tropical dried fruits. From start to finish, this smoothie takes about one hour to prepare, so make sure you don't leave this one until the last minute.

Makes 2 glasses

50g/2oz dried apples
25g/1oz dried apricots
2 fruit teabags
juice of 1 lemon
30ml/2 tbsp crème fraîche or natural (plain) yogurt
mineral water (optional)

3 Put the fruit and tea mixture into a blender or food processor and add the lemon juice. Blend well until smooth, scraping the mixture down from the side of the bowl, if necessary.

Cook's tip
Apple and lemon, apple and mango, forest berries and strawberry and raspberry fruit teas are just a few that are readily available. When choosing the dried fruit, pick the types that will work best with the flavours in your tea.

1 Using a small, sharp knife, roughly chop the dried apples and apricots. Steep the teabags in 300ml/½ pint/ 1¼ cups boiling water for 5 minutes, then remove the teabags.

2 Add the chopped fruit to the tea and leave to stand for 30 minutes. Chill in the refrigerator for about 30 minutes until the tea is completely cold.

4 Add the crème fraîche or yogurt and blend briefly, adding a little mineral water if the smoothie is too thick. Serve in tall glasses.

Very berry

Fresh and frozen cranberries are often in short supply, but dried berries are available all year round and make a tasty dairy-free shake when combined with soya milk. Tiny crimson redcurrants make the perfect partner for the dried cranberries in this refreshingly tart, sparkling smoothie, and this low-fat blend is packed with natural sugars, essential nutrients and vitamins.

Makes 1 large glass

25g/1oz/¼ cup dried cranberries
150g/5oz/1¼ cups redcurrants, plus extra
  to decorate
10ml/2 tsp clear honey
50ml/2fl oz/¼ cup soya milk
sparkling mineral water

1 Put the cranberries in a small bowl, pour over 90ml/6 tbsp boiling water and leave to stand for 10 minutes.

2 String the redcurrants by drawing the stems through the tines of a fork to pull off the delicate currants.

3 Put the currants in a food processor or blender with the cranberries and soaking water. Blend well until smooth.

4 Add the honey and soya milk and whizz briefly to combine the ingredients.

5 Pour the berry shake into a large glass, then top with a little sparkling mineral water to lighten the drink. Drape the redcurrants decoratively over the edge of the glass and serve the smoothie immediately.

Cook's tip
Allowing time for the dried cranberries to rehydrate means they will become plump and juicy – making them much easier to blend and maximizing their flavour.

Purple haze

Thick, dark blueberry purée swirled into pale and creamy vanilla-flavoured buttermilk looks stunning and tastes simply divine. Despite its creaminess, the buttermilk gives this sumptuous smoothie a delicious sharp tang. If you do not like buttermilk or cannot find it in your local supermarket, you could use a mixture of half natural yogurt and half milk instead.

Makes 2 tall glasses

250g/9oz/2¼ cups blueberries
50g/2oz/¼ cup caster (superfine) sugar
15ml/1 tbsp lemon juice
300ml/½ pint/1¼ cups buttermilk
5ml/1 tsp vanilla essence (extract)
150ml/¼ pint/⅔ cup full cream (whole) milk

1 Push the blueberries through a juicer and stir in 15ml/1 tbsp of the sugar and the lemon juice. Stir well and divide between two tall glasses.

2 Put the buttermilk, vanilla essence, milk and remaining sugar in a blender or food processor and blend until really frothy. (Alternatively, use a hand-held electric blender and blend until the mixture froths up.)

3 Pour the buttermilk mixture over the blueberry juice so the mixtures swirl together naturally – there is no need to stir them together as it tastes and looks better if they remain separate to a certain degree. Serve immediately.

Cook's tip
Deep violet blueberry juice makes a fantastic contrast in both colour and flavour to the buttermilk. If you cannot get hold of blueberries, other slightly tart fruits such as raspberries or blackberries would also work in this creamy combination.

Berry smooth

This simple recipe uses oat milk, a cholesterol-free, calcium-rich alternative to cow's milk, and a good partner to sweet summer fruits. Although a good store-cupboard stand-by, you might prefer to keep the oat milk in the refrigerator, ready for an impromptu milkshake whenever you're in the mood. For a really chilled, extremely refreshing flavour, use a mixed bag of semi-thawed frozen fruits, which will blend to a fabulously thick consistency.

Makes 2 glasses

250g/9oz frozen mixed summer fruits,
    partially thawed, plus extra to garnish
130g/4½oz/generous ½ cup soya yogurt
45ml/3 tbsp vanilla syrup
350ml/12fl oz/1½ cups oat milk

Cook's tip
Vanilla syrup is really sweet and full of flavour, great for giving drinks and desserts a deep, mellow flavour. If you cannot find any, use 45ml/3 tbsp caster (superfine) sugar and 5ml/1 tsp good quality vanilla essence (extract).

1 Put the partially thawed mixed summer fruits in a blender or food processor. Add the soya yogurt and blend thoroughly to make a thick purée. Scrape the mixture down from the side of the bowl with a rubber spatula, if necessary, and blend again, briefly, to incorporate into the mixture.

2 Add the vanilla syrup and oat milk to the fruit purée and blend the mixture again until smooth.

3 Transfer the smoothie to a small jug (pitcher) and chill, or pour it into two tall glasses and serve immediately, decorated with the extra fruits.

Pear, rhubarb and cranberry cooler

For best results this delicious smoothie should be made with really ripe and extremely juicy pears, so if the ones you buy are hard, leave them in the fruit bowl for several days before making this fresh and fruity treat. Do not forget to cook the rhubarb well in advance so that it has plenty of time to cool down before you start blending.

Makes 3–4 glasses

400g/14oz early rhubarb
2 large ripe pears
130g/4½oz/generous 1 cup fresh or
    frozen cranberries
90g/3½oz/½ cup caster (superfine) sugar
mineral water (optional)

Cook's tip
If you are using frozen cranberries, don't bother to thaw them first. They'll still blend, and their icy coolness will chill the smoothie to just the right temperature.

1 Using a small, sharp knife, trim the rhubarb and cut into 2cm/¾in lengths.

2 Place the rhubarb slices in a pan with 90ml/6 tbsp water and cover with a tight-fitting lid. Cook gently for about 5 minutes or until tender. Transfer to a bowl and leave to cool, putting several pieces aside for garnish.

3 Peel, quarter and core the pears and tip into a blender or food processor with the cranberries, the rhubarb and its cooking juices and the sugar.

4 Blend until smooth, scraping down the side of the bowl, if necessary. Thin with mineral water, if you like, then serve, garnished with the rhubarb pieces.

Rosemary nectar

This is one of those smoothies that's only worth making if you've got the perfect, ripe ingredients. The fabulously aromatic fragrance of fresh rosemary reacts with the sweet, scented flavour of juicy nectarines to produce a delicious blend with a mouthwatering taste that will almost explode on your tongue – make plenty as you're sure to want more.

Makes 3 glasses

4 long rosemary sprigs, plus extra
   to decorate
15ml/1 tbsp golden caster (superfine) sugar
2.5ml/½ tsp ground ginger
2 oranges
4 nectarines
ice cubes

1 Put the rosemary sprigs in a small pan with the sugar, ground ginger and 150ml/¼ pint/⅔ cup water. Heat gently until the sugar dissolves, then simmer for 1 minute. Remove from the heat, transfer the sprigs and syrup to a bowl and leave to cool.

2 Squeeze the oranges. Halve and stone (pit) the nectarines and put in a food processor or blender with the orange juice. Process until smooth but don't worry if there are a few specks of nectarine skin dotting the juice.

3 Remove the rosemary from the syrup and pour into the juice. Blend briefly.

4 Put a few ice cubes in each glass and fill with the juice. Serve immediately, with extra rosemary sprigs to decorate.

Cook's tip
If you've bought nectarines only to find that they're as hard as bullets, leave them in the fruit bowl for a couple of days – they should ripen fairly quickly.

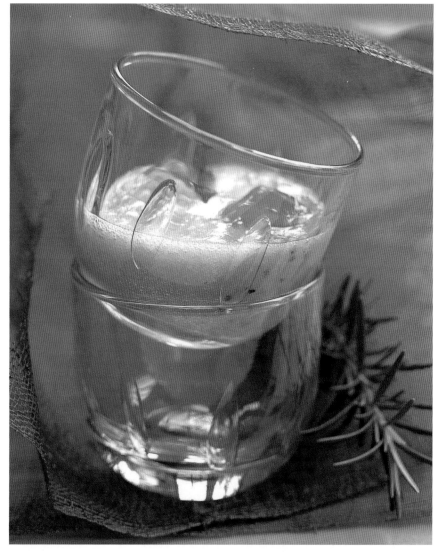

Vanilla snow

While a good quality vanilla essence is perfectly acceptable for flavouring drinks, a far more aromatic taste will be achieved using a vanilla pod. This simple smoothie is deliciously scented, creamy and thick, and well worth the extravagance of using a whole vanilla pod. Its lovely, snowy whiteness is delightfully speckled with tiny black vanilla seeds.

Makes 3 glasses

1 vanilla pod (bean)
25g/1oz/2 tbsp caster (superfine) sugar
3 eating apples
300g/11oz/1⅓ cups natural (plain) yogurt

1 Using the tip of a sharp knife, split open the vanilla pod lengthways. Put it in a small pan with the sugar and 75ml/5 tbsp water. Heat until the sugar dissolves, then boil for 1 minute. Remove from the heat and leave to steep for 10 minutes.

2 Cut the apples into large chunks and push through the juicer, then pour the juice into a large bowl or jug (pitcher).

3 Lift the vanilla pod out of the pan and scrape the tiny black seeds back into the syrup. Pour into the apple juice.

4 Add the yogurt to the bowl or jug and whisk well by hand or with an electric mixer until the smoothie is thick and frothy. Pour into glasses and serve.

Cook's tip
Like most smoothies, this one should ideally be served well chilled. Either use apples and yogurt straight from the refrigerator, or chill briefly before serving. To make a thick, icy version, you could try using frozen yogurt.

Raspberry, apple and rose water smoothie

Although usually put through the juicer for drinking, apples can be blended as long as you process them well to ensure a really flavour-packed smoothie. This recipe is thinned with fresh apple juice, which can be either shop-bought (make sure it is good quality) or home-made.

Makes 2 glasses

2 eating apples
10ml/2 tsp caster (superfine) sugar
15ml/1 tbsp lemon juice
130g/4½oz/¾ cup fresh or frozen raspberries
150ml/¼ pint/⅔ cup apple juice
15–30ml/1–2 tbsp rose water
whole raspberries and rose petals,
    to decorate (optional)

Cook's tip
If you prefer raspberries without the pips (seeds), blend them first and then push the purée through a sieve to remove the pips before mixing it with the apples.

1 Peel and core the apples and put in a blender or food processor with the sugar and lemon juice. Blend well until smooth, scraping the mixture down from the side of the bowl, if necessary.

2 Add the raspberries and apple juice to the apple purée and blend until completely smooth.

3 Add the rose water to the smoothie and blend briefly to combine.

4 Pour the smoothie into two medium glasses and place whole raspberries and rose petals on top of the drinks to decorate, if you like. Serve the smoothie immediately, or chill in the refrigerator until ready to serve.

Coconut and hazelnut smoothie

This intensely nutty, rich and creamy drink is one to sip at your leisure. Leftovers can be put in the refrigerator for up to a couple of days, in which time the flavour of the hazelnuts will develop.

Makes 2 glasses

90g/3½oz/scant 1 cup whole
    blanched hazelnuts
25g/1oz/2 tbsp golden caster
    (superfine) sugar
2.5ml/½ tsp almond essence (extract)
200ml/7fl oz/scant 1 cup coconut cream
30ml/2 tbsp double (heavy) cream (optional)
150ml/¼ pint/⅔ cup mineral water
crushed ice

Cook's tip
If you want a frothy topping on this creamy smoothie, whisk it using a handheld electric wand after adding the mineral water, before pouring into the glasses.

1 Roughly chop the hazelnuts and lightly toast them in a small frying pan, turning frequently. Leave to cool, then tip the nuts into a blender or food processor with the caster sugar and blend well until very finely ground.

2 Add the almond essence, coconut cream and double cream, if using, and blend thoroughly until smooth.

3 Strain the mixture through a sieve into a jug (pitcher), pressing the pulp down with the back of a spoon to extract as much juice as possible. Stir in the mineral water.

4 Half-fill two glasses with crushed ice and pour over the nut smoothie. Serve the drinks immediately, or chill in the refrigerator until ready to serve.

Cinnamon squash

Lightly cooked butternut squash makes a delicious smoothie. It has a wonderfully rich, rounded flavour that is lifted perfectly by the addition of tart citrus juice and warm, spicy cinnamon. Imagine pumpkin pie as a gorgeous smooth drink and you're halfway to experiencing the flavours of this lusciously sweet and tantalizing treat.

2 Put the cooled squash in a blender or food processor and add the ground cinnamon.

3 Squeeze the lemons and grapefruit and pour the juice over the squash, then add the muscovado sugar.

4 Process the ingredients until they are very smooth. If necessary, pause to scrape down the side of the food processor or blender.

5 Put a few ice cubes in two or three short glasses and pour over the smoothie. Serve immediately.

Makes 2–3 glasses

1 small butternut squash,
   about 600g/1lb 6oz
2.5ml/½ tsp ground cinnamon
3 large lemons
1 grapefruit
60ml/4 tbsp light muscovado (brown) sugar
ice cubes

Cook's tip
If you can only buy a large squash, cook it all and add the leftovers to stew or soup.

1 Halve the squash, scoop out and discard the seeds and cut the flesh into chunks. Cut away the skin and discard. Steam or boil the squash for 10–15 minutes until just tender. Drain well and leave to stand until cool.

Green devil

Choose a well-flavoured avocado, such as a knobbly, dark-skinned Haas, for this slightly spicy, hot and sour smoothie. Cucumber adds a refreshing edge, while lemon and lime juice zip up the flavour, and the chilli sauce adds an irresistible fiery bite. This is one little devil that is sure to liven up even the most lethargic days.

Makes 2–3 glasses

1 small ripe avocado
½ cucumber
30ml/2 tbsp lemon juice
30ml/2 tbsp lime juice
10ml/2 tsp caster (superfine) sugar
pinch of salt
250ml/8fl oz/1 cup apple juice or
   mineral water
10–20ml/2–4 tsp sweet chilli sauce
ice cubes
red chilli curls, to decorate

1 Halve the avocado and use a sharp knife to remove the stone (pit). Scoop the flesh from both halves into a blender or food processor. Peel and roughly chop the cucumber and add to the blender or food processor, then add the lemon and lime juice, the caster sugar and a little salt.

Cook's tip
To make chilli curls, core and seed a fresh red chilli and cut it into very fine strips. Put the strips in a bowl of iced water and leave to stand for 20 minutes or until the strips curl. Use them to decorate this smoothie.

   Seductively smooth avocados are as good for you as they taste. Their fresh vitamin- and mineral-rich flesh is reputed to be fantastic for healthy hair and skin.

2 Process the ingredients until smooth and creamy, then add the apple juice or mineral water and a little of the chilli sauce. Blend once more to lightly mix the ingredients together.

3 Pour the smoothie over ice cubes. Decorate with red chilli curls and serve with stirrers and extra chilli sauce.

Red defender

Boost your body's defences with this delicious blend of red fruits. Watermelon and strawberries are a good source of vitamin C and the black watermelon seeds, like all other seeds, are rich in essential nutrients. If you really don't like the idea of blending the seeds, remove them first.

1 Hull the strawberries and halve them if they are large. Pull the grapes from their stalks. Cut away the skin from the watermelon.

2 Put the watermelon in a blender or food processor and blend until the seeds are broken up. Add the strawberries and grapes and blend until completely smooth, scraping the mixture down from the side of the bowl, if necessary. Serve in tall glasses.

Makes 2 glasses

200g/7oz/1¾ cups strawberries
small bunch red grapes, about 90g/3½oz
1 small wedge of watermelon

Cook's tip
Decorate this juice with chunks of watermelon or strawberry halves.

Apricot squash

The availability of fresh apricots can be rather erratic, so buy lots when you see them and make delicious apricot-based juices like this one. Choose sweet and juicy, ripe apricots, as they will act as a perfect foil to the tangy limes in this refreshing drink.

Makes 2 glasses

2 limes
3 oranges
4 ripe apricots
several sprigs of lemon balm, plus extra
     to decorate

Cook's tip
This makes a tangy, invigorating blend to wake up your senses. Stir in a little honey or sugar if you find it a bit too tart.

1 Squeeze the limes and oranges, either by hand or using a citrus juicer. Halve and stone (pit) the apricots.

2 Put the apricots in a blender or food processor with a little of the citrus juice and the lemon balm, and blend until smooth, scraping the mixture down from the side of the bowl, if necessary. Add the remaining juice and blend until completely smooth.

3 Pour into medium glasses and serve decorated with extra lemon balm.

Thyme-scented plum lush

Make this divine drink in the early autumn when plums are at their sweetest and best. Their silky smooth flesh blends down to produce the most wonderfully textured smoothie, while delicately scented lemon thyme and honey complement the flavour perfectly. This luxurious juice is easy to make and has an irresistible fragrance that is at once warming and refreshing.

Makes 2–3 glasses

400g/14oz red plums
30–45ml/2–3 tbsp clear honey
15ml/1 tbsp chopped fresh lemon thyme,
    plus extra thyme sprigs to decorate
100g/3¾oz crushed ice

Cook's tip
Dark, purplish-red plums, with their almost violet bloom and sweet, intense flavour, juice well and make some of the most tempting and vibrant fruit drinks.

1 Using a sharp knife, halve and stone (pit) the plums and put in a blender or food processor. Add 30ml/2 tbsp of the honey and the lemon thyme and blend until smooth, scraping down the side of the bowl, if necessary.

2 Add the ice and blend until slushy. Taste for sweetness, adding a little more honey if necessary. Pour into glasses and serve immediately, decorated with a sprig of thyme.

Fire and ice

Tickle your tastebuds with this unconventional frozen yogurt drink that is flavoured with fresh orange juice and specks of hot red chilli. It's great on a hot summer's day, after lunch or any other time when you're in need of a refreshing boost. If you've plenty of time on your hands, add an alcoholic kick to the drink by drizzling each glass with a splash of orange liqueur before serving.

Makes 2–3 tall glasses

90g/3½oz/½ cup caster (superfine) sugar
1 lemon
300ml/½ pint/1¼ cups freshly squeezed
    orange juice
200g/7oz/scant 1 cup Greek (US strained
    plain) yogurt
1 red chilli, seeded and finely chopped
60ml/4 tbsp Cointreau or other orange-
    flavoured liqueur (optional)
orange slices and extra chillies, to decorate

1 Put the sugar in a pan with 100ml/ 3½fl oz/scant ½ cup water and heat gently, stirring with a spoon until the sugar has dissolved. Pour into a freezer container and leave to cool. Finely grate the rind of the lemon and juice.

2 Add the lemon rind and juice and 100ml/3½fl oz/scant ½ cup of the orange juice. Freeze for 2 hours or until a band of ice has formed around the edges. Turn into a bowl and add the yogurt and chopped chilli. Whisk until thick. Freeze for 1–2 hours until almost solid.

3 To serve, scoop the frozen yogurt into a blender or food processor and add the remaining orange juice. Process until very thick and smooth. Pour into tall glasses and drizzle with a little liqueur, if using. Serve with straws and decorate with orange slices and fresh chillies.

Cook's tip

Don't worry if you forget to remove the chilli yogurt from the freezer before it has frozen solid. Leave it at room temperature for a while to soften or simply heat it briefly in a microwave.

cool
creamy
shakes

Milkshakes can be either refreshing and fruity or smooth and creamy, but they are always a treat. Inspiring ingredients include brownies and garden mint, and there are several shakes made with more traditional flavours such as vanilla or banana. Fun for kids and nostalgically appealing for adults, comfort drinks never looked or tasted so good.

Real vanilla milkshake

This is a milkshake for connoisseurs: it is the cream of the crop and definitely one to linger over. Nothing beats the flavour achieved by infusing a vanilla pod in the milk beforehand, but if you just cannot wait for the milk to cool, use a teaspoon of good quality vanilla essence instead.

Makes 2 glasses

1 vanilla pod (bean)
400ml/14fl oz/1⅔ cups full cream
   (whole) milk
200ml/7fl oz/scant 1 cup single (light) cream
4 scoops vanilla ice cream

1 Using a sharp knife, score the vanilla pod down the centre. Place in a small pan, pour the milk over and bring slowly to the boil.

2 Remove the pan from the heat but leave the pod in the milk. Leave to stand until the milk has cooled.

3 Remove the vanilla pod from the cooled milk and scrape out the seeds with the tip of a knife. Put the seeds in a blender or food processor with the milk and cream. Blend until combined.

4 Add the vanilla ice cream to the mixture and blend well until it is deliciously thick and frothy. Pour the smoothie into two large glasses and serve immediately with stirrers and straws to decorate, if you like.

Cook's tip
This classic milkshake is extremely rich and creamy, but if you'd prefer a lighter consistency, replace half the cream with the same quantity of extra milk.

Simply strawberry

Nothing evokes a sense of summer wellbeing more than the scent and flavour of sweet, juicy strawberries. This recipe uses an abundance of these fragrant fruits so, if possible, make it when the season is right and local ones are at their most plentiful.

Makes 2 glasses

400g/14oz/3½ cups strawberries, plus extra
   to decorate
30–45ml/2–3 tbsp icing (confectioners') sugar
200g/7oz/scant 1 cup Greek (US strained
   plain) yogurt
60ml/4 tbsp single (light) cream

Cook's tip
You can replace the strawberries with other fruits if they are not in season. Try using fresh bananas instead to make another very popular milkshake.

1 Hull the strawberries and place them in a blender or food processor with 30ml/2 tbsp of the icing sugar. Blend to a smooth purée, scraping the mixture down from the side of the bowl with a rubber spatula, if necessary.

2 Add the yogurt and cream and blend again until smooth and frothy. Check the sweetness, adding a little more sugar if you find the flavour too sharp. Pour into glasses and serve decorated with extra strawberries.

Rose petal and almond milk

If you're lucky enough to have a mass of roses in the garden, it's well worth sacrificing a few to make this delicately scented summer smoothie. Thickened and flavoured with ground ratafia biscuits, this fragrant drink is the perfect way to relax on a hot lazy afternoon.

Makes 2 glasses

15g/½oz scented rose petals (preferably
    pink), plus extra to decorate
300ml/½ pint/1¼ cups milk
25g/1oz ratafia biscuits (almond macaroons)
ice cubes

Cook's tip
If you have bought roses, or even if you have picked them from your own garden, make sure you wash the petals thoroughly before you use them for cooking. This will help to remove any chemicals or pesticides that may have been sprayed on to the flowers.

1 Put the rose petals in a small pan with half the milk and bring just to the boil. Put the ratafia biscuits in a bowl, pour over the hot milk and leave to stand for 10 minutes.

2 Transfer the mixture to a blender or food processor with the remaining milk, and blend until smooth.

3 Strain the milk through a sieve into a wide jug (pitcher) to remove any lumps of biscuit or rose petals that have not been blended properly, and chill for at least 1 hour.

4 When the milk is well chilled, pour over ice cubes and serve immediately, decorating with rose petals, if you like.

Banana and maple crunch

Brilliant for making quick and easy blended drinks, bananas have a natural affinity with maple syrup and pecan nuts – what a combination. Serve this creamy, syrupy smoothie over ice and, if you are feeling decadent, dunk in some chunky chocolate cookies to scoop up a mouthful. It is best to serve this smoothie as soon as it is ready because it will not keep well. Finishing it off in one sitting should not be too difficult.

Makes 2 glasses

2 large bananas
50g/2oz/½ cup pecan nuts, plus extra to serve
150ml/¼ pint/⅔ cup full cream (whole) milk
60ml/4 tbsp pure maple syrup
crushed ice

Cook's tips
It is important to use ripe bananas in this recipe and, although you could replace the nuts with another variety such as hazelnuts, the combination of pecans, bananas and maple syrup is such a classic that any variation won't be as good.

1 Put the bananas in a blender or food processor and process until smooth. Add the nuts and blend again until thoroughly combined.

2 The nuts must be finely ground so stop and scrape down the side of the bowl once or twice, if necessary.

3 Add the maple syrup, then pour the milk over the banana paste and blend again until creamy.

4 Half-fill two large glasses with crushed ice and pour the smoothie over the top. Serve sprinkled with extra pecan nuts, if you like.

Honey and banana milkshake

This delicious drink demonstrates just how smooth and creamy a milkshake can be, even without using dairy produce. Make it using either soya or rice milk together with a vanilla-flavoured, iced non-dairy dessert to achieve a surprisingly rich and creamy flavour. Bananas make a nutritious, energy-boosting addition to drinks – this one is almost a meal in itself.

Makes 2 glasses

2 bananas
30ml/2 tbsp clear honey
15ml/1 tbsp lemon juice
300ml/½ pint/1¼ cups soya or rice milk
4 scoops vanilla iced non-dairy dessert

Cook's tip
If you are happy to use dairy produce, simply use ordinary milk and vanilla ice cream in place of the non-dairy ingredients.

1 Break the bananas into pieces and put in a blender or food processor with the honey and lemon juice. Blend until very smooth, scraping the mixture down from the side of the bowl with a rubber spatula, if necessary.

2 Add the soya or rice milk and two scoops of iced non-dairy dessert, then blend until smooth. Pour into tall glasses and add another scoop of dessert to each. Serve immediately.

Stem ginger and pear shake

Although fresh fruit cannot be beaten for its flavour and nutritional value, canned varieties are a good store-cupboard stand-by for when you've run out of fresh. They are still nutritionally sound, particularly if packed in natural, unsweetened fruit juice. Preserved stem ginger makes the perfect partner to pears in this taste-tingling, creamy creation.

1 Shave off some wafer-thin slices from one of the pieces of ginger and reserve. Roughly chop the remaining ginger. Drain the pears, reserving about 150ml/¼ pint/⅔ cup of the juice.

2 Put the pears, measured juice and chopped ginger in a blender or food processor and blend until smooth, scraping the mixture down from the side of the bowl, if necessary.

3 Strain through a sieve into a jug (pitcher). Whisk in the milk, cream and ginger syrup and pour into two glasses. Serve scattered with the ginger shavings.

Makes 2 glasses

3 pieces (about 65g/2½oz) preserved stem
   ginger, plus 30ml/2 tbsp ginger syrup from
   the jar
400g/14oz can pears in natural fruit juice
150ml/¼ pint/⅔ cup full cream (whole) milk
100ml/3½fl oz/scant ½ cup single
   (light) cream
ice cubes

Cook's tip
If you like your milkshake really smooth, strain the pear mixture through a sieve to remove any bits of fibre that might remain in the pears. However, if you like the consistency of the stringy bits, skip this part of the recipe.

Lemon meringue

Just as lemon meringue pie is a favourite dessert, this wonderful milkshake is sure to become a favourite drink. The blend of sweet meringue and lemon is carefully balanced in a velvety smooth, ice-cool drink that is not too rich and surprisingly refreshing. This really is a dessert in a glass and will undoubtedly go down well at your next dinner party.

2 Coarsely crush 15g/½oz of the meringues and reserve for decoration. Break the remainder into a blender or food processor. Add the lemon syrup and blend until smooth.

3 With the machine still running, gradually pour in the milk until the mixture is pale and frothy. Add the ice cream and blend again until smooth.

4 Pour the milkshake into tall glasses and decorate the sides with lemon slices or twists of lemon peel. Scatter the reserved meringue on top and serve immediately with spoons.

Makes 2 glasses

30ml/2 tbsp caster (superfine) sugar
3 lemons
50g/2oz crisp white meringues
300ml/½ pint/1¼ cups full cream (whole) milk
2 scoops vanilla ice cream
lemon slices or twists of peel,
    to decorate

Cook's tip
When shopping for the lemons to decorate this drink, be sure to buy the unwaxed variety.

1 Put the sugar in a small pan with 100ml/3½fl oz/scant ½ cup water and heat gently until the sugar dissolves. Pour into a jug (pitcher). Squeeze the lemons using a citrus juicer and add the juice to the syrup. Leave to cool.

Garden mint milkshake

If you have mint growing in your garden, pick some for this recipe, as the fresher the mint, the better the flavour will be. The mint is infused in a sugar syrup, then left to cool before being blended to an aromatic, frothy shake with yogurt and creamy milk. The final milkshake is speckled with tiny green flecks, but if you prefer a completely smooth texture, you can strain these out.

Makes 2 tall glasses

25g/1oz/1 cup fresh mint
50g/2oz/¼ cup caster (superfine) sugar
200g/7oz/scant 1 cup natural
   (plain) yogurt
200ml/7fl oz/scant 1 cup full cream
   (whole) milk
15ml/1 tbsp lemon juice
crushed ice cubes
icing (confectioners') sugar, to decorate

2 Heat the mixture, stirring occasionally, until the sugar dissolves, then boil for 2 minutes. Remove the pan from the heat and set aside until the syrup is completely cool.

3 Strain the cooled syrup through a sieve into a jug (pitcher), pressing the mint against the side of the sieve with the back of a spoon. Pour into a blender or food processor.

4 Add the yogurt and milk to the syrup and blend until smooth and frothy. Add two of the reserved mint sprigs and the lemon juice and blend until the milkshake is specked with tiny green flecks.

5 Put the crushed ice in tall glasses or tumblers and pour over the milkshake. Dust the mint sprigs with icing sugar and use to decorate the glasses. Serve.

1 Pull out four small mint sprigs and set aside. Roughly snip the remaining leaves into a small pan. Add the sugar and pour over 105ml/7 tbsp water.

Rosemary and almond cream

This delightful concoction is definitely one to choose if you are looking for something a little different. Fresh sprigs of rosemary, infused in milk, provide a gentle fragrance and flavour that blends deliciously with the sweet ratafia biscuits. Frothed up with creamy, melting vanilla ice cream, this velvety smooth creation is quite simply superb.

Makes 2 glasses

4 long sprigs of fresh rosemary
400ml/14fl oz/1⅔ cups full cream (whole) milk
50g/2oz ratafia biscuits (almond macaroons) or amaretti, plus extra to decorate
3 large scoops vanilla ice cream
frosted rosemary sprigs, to decorate

Cook's tip
To make frosted rosemary sprigs, lightly coat the sprigs in a little beaten egg white. Dip in caster (superfine) sugar and leave to dry.

1 Put the rosemary sprigs in a small pan. Add 150ml/¼ pint/⅔ cup of the milk and heat very gently until the milk begins to boil. Remove the pan from the heat and tip the mixture into a bowl. Leave to cool for 10 minutes.

2 Remove the rosemary sprigs and carefully pour the still warm milk into a blender or food processor. Add the ratafia biscuits and blend until smooth and creamy. Add the remaining 250ml/8fl oz/1 cup milk and blend the mixture thoroughly.

3 Scoop the vanilla ice cream into the milk and biscuit mixture and blend until it is fully incorporated. Pour into large glasses and serve the milkshake immediately, decorating the top of each glass with delicate frosted rosemary sprigs and a few pieces of crumbled ratafia biscuits.

Pistachio thick-shake

Don't be put off by the presence of rice in this lovely, layered dairy-free milkshake. Blended with soya milk, pistachio nuts and non-dairy ice cream, it makes a dreamy, creamy blend that can be sipped, layer by layer, or swirled together with a pretty stirrer. As its name suggests, this shake is wonderfully rich and decadent; serve it in tall narrow glasses.

Makes 3–4 small glasses

550ml/18fl oz/2½ cups soya milk
50g/2oz/generous ¼ cup pudding rice
60ml/4 tbsp caster (superfine) sugar
finely grated rind of 1 lemon
75g/3oz/¾ cup shelled pistachio nuts, plus extra to decorate
300ml/10fl oz vanilla iced non-dairy dessert
5ml/1 tsp almond essence (extract)

1 Put the soya milk in a large, heavy pan with the rice, sugar and lemon rind. Bring slowly to the boil, then reduce the heat to simmer. Partially cover the pan with a lid and cook on the lowest heat for about 30 minutes, or until the rice is completely tender.

2 Transfer the rice to a heatproof bowl and leave to stand until completely cold.

3 Put the pistachio nuts in another heatproof bowl and cover with boiling water. Leave to stand for about 2 minutes and then drain.

4 Rub the pistachio nuts between several layers of kitchen paper to loosen the skins, then peel them away. (Don't worry about removing every bit of skin, but getting most of it off will make a prettier coloured milkshake.)

5 Tip the cold rice into a blender or food processor and blend until smooth. Put half the mixture in a bowl. Add the non-dairy dessert to the blender and blend until smooth. Pour into a separate bowl. Add the nuts, the reserved rice and the almond essence to the blender and process until the nuts are finely ground.

6 Layer the two mixtures in glasses and serve decorated with extra pistachios.

Marzipan and orange crush

The wintry scents and flavours of juicy oranges and marzipan make an interesting combination and the citrus juice adds a delicious refreshing tang to an otherwise very rich, creamy drink. It's a great blend to make if you are entertaining friends as its unusual blend of ingredients is sure to be a talking point. Make plenty of this irresistible shake and chill whatever you don't use in the refrigerator for another time.

Makes 3–4 glasses

130g/4½oz marzipan
finely grated rind and juice of 2 large oranges
juice of 1 lemon
150ml/¼ pint/⅔ cup mineral water
150ml/¼ pint/⅔ cup single (light) cream
ice cubes
orange wedges, to decorate (optional)

Cook's tip
Give this drink a whisk before serving, as it may have settled.

1 Break the marzipan into small pieces and put in a blender or food processor. Add the orange rind and juice along with the lemon juice. Blend the mixture thoroughly until smooth.

2 Add the mineral water and cream and blend again until smooth and frothy. Pour over ice cubes in glasses and serve decorated with the orange wedges, if you like.

Cherry and coconut shake

The season for fresh cherries is all too short, but canned cherries make a very good and surprisingly delicious stand-by. Here they are combined in a classic partnership with creamy coconut milk to make a rich, fruity drink that is perfect for people who are not too keen on really sweet, thick milkshakes. Make sure you buy pitted cherries, otherwise you will have to carefully stone them yourself before tipping them into the blender.

Makes 2 glasses

425g/15oz can pitted black cherries
   in syrup
200ml/7fl oz/scant 1 cup coconut milk
15ml/1 tbsp light muscovado (brown) sugar
150ml/¼ pint/⅔ cup black cherry-flavour
   yogurt
100ml/3½fl oz/scant ½ cup double
   (heavy) cream
lightly toasted shredded coconut,
   to decorate

Cook's tip
If you can't get black cherry flavour yogurt, use a vanilla or natural (plain) yogurt instead and add a little extra sugar when blending.

1 Tip the canned cherries into a sieve over a bowl to drain. Reserve the syrup for later.

2 Put the drained cherries in a blender or food processor with the coconut milk and sugar and blend briefly until fairly smooth. (Do not be tempted to over-blend the mixture or it may begin to separate.)

3 Pour the mixture through a sieve into a jug (pitcher), pressing the pulp down into the sieve with the back of a spoon to extract as much juice as possible.

4 Add the reserved cherry syrup, yogurt and cream and whisk lightly until smooth and frothy. Pour into glasses and scatter with shredded coconut.

Passionata

The combination of ripe passion fruit with sweet caramel is gorgeous in this dreamy milkshake. For convenience, you can easily make the caramel syrup and combine it with the fresh passion fruit juice in advance, so it's all ready for blending with the milk. For the best results make sure you use really ripe, crinkly passion fruit.

Makes 4 glasses

90g/3½oz/½ cup caster (superfine) sugar
juice of 2 large oranges
juice of 1 lemon
6 ripe passion fruit, plus extra for garnish
550ml/18fl oz/2½ cups full cream
    (whole) milk
ice cubes

1 Put the sugar in a small, heavy pan with 200ml/7fl oz/scant 1 cup water. Heat gently, stirring with a wooden spoon until the sugar has dissolved.

2 Bring the mixture to the boil and cook, without stirring, for about 5 minutes until the syrup has turned to a deep golden caramel. Watch closely towards the end of the cooking time as caramel can burn very quickly. If this happens, let the caramel cool, then throw it away and start again.

3 When the caramel has turned deep golden, immediately lower the base of the pan into cold water to prevent it from cooking any further.

4 Carefully add the orange and lemon juice, standing back slightly as the mixture will splutter. Return the pan to the heat and cook gently, stirring continuously, to make a smooth syrup. Transfer the syrup to a small heatproof bowl and set aside until it has cooled completely.

5 Halve the passion fruit and scoop the seeds into a blender or food processor. Add the caramel and milk and blend until smooth and frothy. Pour over ice and serve with a passion fruit garnish.

Rocky river

This rich, sweet milkshake combines chilled custard with decadent chocolate, chunky nuts and delicious marshmallows. It is great fun to make with children, who will enjoy its sticky, indulgent sweetness almost as much as the adults. Prepare this shake whenever you're really in need of a treat or when relaxing in the garden on a hot afternoon.

Makes 3 glasses

75g/3oz plain (semisweet) chocolate
40g/1½oz/scant ½ cup blanched almonds
50g/2oz pink and white marshmallows
600ml/1 pint/2½ cups good quality
   ready-made custard
300ml/½ pint/1¼ cups milk
30ml/2 tbsp caster (superfine) sugar
5ml/1 tsp vanilla essence (extract)

1 Coarsely grate the chocolate. Lightly toast the almonds, then chop them. Cut the marshmallows roughly into pieces, using scissors, reserving a few pieces for decoration.

2 Tip the custard into a blender or food processor and add the milk, sugar and vanilla essence. Blend briefly to combine.

3 Reserve a little chocolate for sprinkling, then add the remainder to the blender with the almonds and marshmallows. Blend until the marshmallows are chopped into small pieces.

4 Pour into big glasses and serve immediately, sprinkled with the reserved marshmallows and grated chocolate.

Cook's tip
Very cold chocolate can be difficult to grate. You might find it easier if you microwave it, very briefly, as this will make the chocolate less brittle for grating.

Cinnamon iced coffee

When the weather warms up, swap mugs of hot coffee for this treat of a summer cooler. Lightly flavoured with cinnamon and served icy cold, it's a smooth relaxing drink for when you need to unwind – and it's well worth keeping a jug in the refrigerator.

Makes 2 large glasses

5ml/1 tsp ground cinnamon
400ml/14fl oz/1⅔ cups full cream (whole) milk
40g/1½oz/3 tbsp caster (superfine) sugar
300ml/½ pint/1¼ cups strong cold espresso coffee
ice cubes
cinnamon sticks, to serve

Cook's tip
For a dinner party, why not spice things up and serve these shakes with a large dash of Bailey's or Tia Maria. These types of alcohol work particularly well with this drink's creaminess and its subtle cinnamon tones.

1 Put the cinnamon and 100ml/3½fl oz/ scant ½ cup of the milk in a small pan with the sugar. Bring the milk slowly to the boil then remove from the heat and leave to cool.

2 Turn the cinnamon milk into a large jug (pitcher) or bowl. Add the remaining milk and the coffee and whisk well, using a hand-held electric wand, until frothy. Pour into glasses with ice and serve with cinnamon sticks for stirrers.

Chocolate brownie milkshake

For a truly indulgent flavour, use home-made chocolate brownies in this fabulously tasty milkshake. It is very rich – and incredibly decadent – so sit back, relax and just enjoy a totally luxurious moment on your own – well, you wouldn't want to share it.

1 Crumble the chocolate brownies into a blender or food processor and add the milk. Blend until the mixture is a pale chocolate colour.

2 Add the ice cream and blend until smooth and frothy. Pour into a tall glass and spoon over a little whipped cream. Serve scattered with chocolate shavings or a dusting of cocoa powder.

Makes 1 large glass

40g/1½oz chocolate brownies
200ml/7fl oz/scant 1 cup full cream
　(whole) milk
2 scoops vanilla ice cream
a little whipped cream
chocolate shavings or cocoa powder
　(unsweetened), to decorate

Cook's tip
If you fancy treating yourself to a milkshake that's even more chocolatey than this one, replace the vanilla ice cream with the same amount of a chocolate or chocolate-chip variety.

drinks
for
kids

Drinks for breakfast, after school or even kids'
parties are transformed with these delicious
concoctions. There are fresh fruit smoothies, fun
floats and shakes, and some real tea-time treats
that could quite easily take the place of an ordinary
dessert or pudding. Let the kids help prepare them
and they'll enjoy these blends even more.

Raspberry, banana and peach smoothie

Children will love this naturally sweet fruit drink. Whizzed up in just minutes, this thick, slightly tart smoothie makes a good stop-gap between meals, a brilliant, easy-to-eat breakfast or serves as a healthy – and very tasty – dessert.

1 Halve, stone (pit) and roughly chop the peach, break the banana into pieces and put both fruits in a blender or food processor. Blend until smooth, scraping the mixture down the side of the bowl if necessary.

2 Add the raspberries and blend until smooth. Pour into glasses and top up with mineral water, if using. Add ice cubes, decorate with extra raspberries and serve with straws or spoons.

Makes 2 small glasses

1 large ripe peach
1 small banana
130g/4½oz/¾ cup fresh or frozen
   raspberries, plus extra to decorate
still or sparkling mineral water (optional)
ice cubes

Cook's tip
If your children are fussy about the pips (seeds) in raspberries, blend them first and push the mixture through a fine sieve to remove the seeds, then return the purée to the blended banana mixture.

Top pops

Chunky ice-lolly stirrers give this fruit-packed smoothie plenty of child-appeal. It's great for a party or as an after-school treat on a hot day. The lollies can be frozen ahead and stored so they're ready on demand, and the juice takes just moments to prepare.

Makes 2 glasses

1 apple
300ml/½ pint/1¼ cups apple juice
2 kiwi fruit
90g/3½oz/generous ½ cup raspberries
10ml/2 tsp caster (superfine) sugar
150g/5oz/1 cup red grapes
150g/5oz/1¼ cups blackcurrants or
  blackberries
1 large banana

1 Peel, core and roughly chop the apple. Place in a food processor or blender with 100ml/3½fl oz/ scant ½ cup of the apple juice and blend to a smooth purée. Pour into a third of the sections of an ice-cube tray.

2 Peel and roughly chop the kiwi fruit and blend until smooth with 100ml of the apple juice. Pour into another third of the ice-cube tray sections.

3 Blend the raspberries with the sugar and the remaining apple juice and spoon into the final sections. Freeze the tray for about 30 minutes then push a wooden ice-lolly (popsicle) stick into each. Freeze until solid.

4 Put the grapes, blackcurrants or blackberries, and banana into the blender or food processor and blend until smooth. If you like, push the mixture through a coarse sieve after blending to remove the seeds and skins.

5 Push several of the fruit lollies out of the tray and place on separate plates for each child. Pour the fruit juice into two glasses and place on plates with the lollies. Serve immediately as the lollies will start to melt very quickly – and don't forget to supply the children with plenty of napkins.

Tropical fruit shake

Sweet, fruity and packed with vitamin C, this is a brilliant way to get children to enjoy healthy drinks. If you use really ripe fruit, it shouldn't need any additional sweetening, but taste it to check before serving. Mango makes a thick purée when blended, so top it up with mineral water – or try a good quality lemonade instead.

Makes 2 glasses

½ small pineapple
small bunch seedless white grapes
1 mango
mineral water or lemonade (optional)

1 Using a sharp knife, cut away the skin from the pineapple and halve the fruit. Discard the core and roughly chop the flesh of one half. Add to a blender or food processor with the grapes. Halve the mango either side of the flat stone (pit). Scoop the flesh into the blender.

2 Process thoroughly until really smooth, scraping the mixture down from the side of the bowl, if necessary. Pour into glasses and top up with mineral water or lemonade, if using. Serve immediately.

Cook's tip
For really fussy children, you might want to strain the mixture first. To do this, push it through a fine sieve, pressing the pulp in the sieve with the back of a spoon to extract as much juice as possible. Follow the recipe as normal, topping up the glasses with mineral water or lemonade if your children prefer it. To make a novelty decoration, thread pieces of fruit on to straws before you serve the shake.

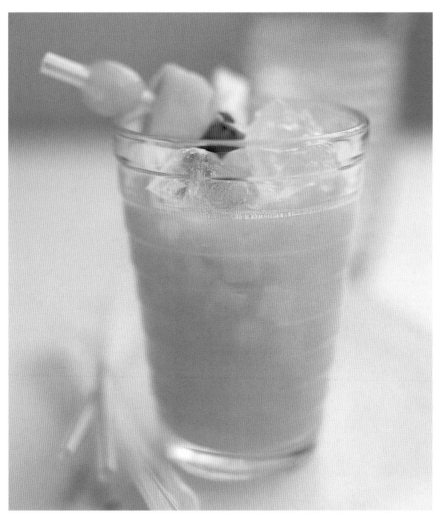

Raspberry rippler

Colourful ripples of raspberry and mango give instant child appeal to this fruit-packed smoothie. Soya milk is so delicious and such a healthy alternative to cow's milk in drinks that it's worth trying, even for children who are not on a dairy-free diet. Here it's blended with mango to create a smooth, thick contrast to the tangy raspberries. For best results, use only really ripe, sweet mango.

Makes 2 glasses

90g/3½oz/generous ½ cup fresh or frozen
   raspberries, plus a few extra to decorate
15–30ml/1–2 tbsp clear honey
1 mango
100ml/3½fl oz/scant ½ cup soya milk

1 Process the raspberries in a blender or food processor until smooth. Add 15ml/1 tbsp water and 5–10ml/1–2 tsp of the honey to sweeten. Transfer to a small bowl and rinse out the blender or food processor bowl.

2 Halve the mango either side of the flat stone (pit). Scoop the flesh from the two halves and around the stone into the clean blender or food processor and process until smooth. Add the soya milk and 10–20ml/2–4 tsp honey to sweeten.

Cook's tip

It will make such a difference to your children's health, and to their general appreciation of food, if they can enjoy fresh, naturally sweet drinks like this. Try serving this smoothie as a refreshing dessert after a barbecue or a family meal – it makes a delicious alternative to the similarly named, but slightly less healthy, raspberry ripple ice cream.

3 Pour a 2.5cm/1in layer of the mango purée into two tumblers. Spoon half the raspberry purée on top. Add the remaining mango purée, then finish with the remaining raspberry purée. Using a teaspoon, lightly swirl the two mixtures together. Serve decorated with extra raspberries.

Candystripe

This wickedly indulgent drink combines freshly blended strawberries with a marshmallow flavoured cream, making a milkshake that adults as well as kids will find totally irresistible. There's no point even trying to resist the melting marshmallow sweetness of this cheeky little strawberry confection – just sit back and give yourself up.

Makes 4 large glasses

150g/5oz white and pink marshmallows
500ml/17fl oz/generous 2 cups full cream
   (whole) milk
60ml/4 tbsp redcurrant jelly
450g/1lb/4 cups strawberries
60ml/4 tbsp double (heavy) cream
extra strawberries and marshmallows,
   to decorate

1 Put the marshmallows in a heavy pan with half the milk and heat gently, stirring frequently until the marshmallows have melted. Leave to stand until it has cooled.

2 Heat the redcurrant jelly in a small pan until melted. Put the strawberries in a blender or food processor and process until smooth, scraping down the side of the bowl with a rubber spatula as often as is necessary.

3 Stir 10ml/2 tsp of the strawberry purée into the melted jelly. Set aside the strawberry syrup. Pour the remaining purée into a jug (pitcher) and add the marshmallow mixture, the cream and the remaining milk. Chill the milkshake and four large glasses for about 1 hour.

4 To serve, use a teaspoon to drizzle lines of the strawberry syrup down the insides of the glasses – this creates a candystripe effect when filled. Fill the glasses with the milkshake. Serve topped with the extra marshmallows and strawberries and drizzle with any leftover strawberry syrup.

Cook's tip
If you can convince the children to wait long enough, this blend will really benefit from being chilled in the refrigerator for a couple of hours before serving.

Peppermint crush

The next time you see seaside rock or the peppermint candy canes that are around at Christmas time, buy a few sticks for this incredibly easy, fun drink for children. All you need to do is whizz it up with some milk and freeze until slushy, so it's ready and waiting for thirsty youngsters. This shake could almost pass as a dessert, so try serving it after a meal.

Makes 4 glasses

90g/3½oz pink peppermint rock (rock candy)
750ml/1¼ pints/3 cups full cream (whole) or
    semi-skimmed (low-fat) milk
a few drops of pink food colouring (optional)
pink candy canes, to serve

Cook's tip
If you cannot find pink candy canes to use as novelty stirrers for this drink, buy peppermint lolly pops instead.

1 While the rock is still in its wrapper, hit with a rolling pin to break into small bits. (If unwrapped, put the rock in a polythene bag to crush it.) Tip the pieces into a blender or food processor.

2 Add the milk and a few drops of pink food colouring, if using, to the crushed rock and process until the rock is broken up into tiny pieces.

3 Pour the mixture into a shallow freezer container and freeze for about 2 hours or until turning slushy around the edges. Beat the mixture with a fork, breaking up the semi-frozen areas and stirring them into the centre.

4 Re-freeze and repeat the process once or twice more until the mixture is slushy. Spoon into glasses and serve with candy cane stirrers.

Custard cream float

This fabulously frothy dessert drink makes a wonderful treat that rounds off any meal brilliantly, or you could serve it to your children as a special snack mid-morning or at teatime.

Makes 3 glasses

75g/3oz custard cream biscuits (cookies)
1 large banana
5ml/1 tsp vanilla essence (extract)
200ml/7fl oz/scant 1 cup full cream (whole) milk
6 scoops vanilla ice cream
banana slices and crumbled biscuit (cookie), to decorate
drinking chocolate or cocoa powder (unsweetened), for dusting

Cook's tip
For an extra burst of banana flavour, use banana ice cream.

1 Put the custard cream biscuits in a blender or food processor and blend well until finely ground. Break the banana into chunks and add to the ground biscuits. Process thoroughly until a smooth, thick paste forms, scraping down the side of the bowl with a rubber spatula, if necessary.

2 Add the vanilla essence, milk and three scoops of the ice cream and process again until smooth and foamy. Pour into tumblers and top with the remaining scoops of ice cream. Decorate with banana slices and crumbled biscuit and serve dusted with a little drinking chocolate or cocoa powder.

Chocolate nut swirl

Children everywhere will be captivated by this fabulous chocolatey concoction. It is a mixture of melted milk chocolate, chocolate nut spread and creamy milk, marbled together to make an attractive and delicious drink. Adults who like chocolate will love it too.

Makes 2 tall glasses

40g/1½oz/3 tbsp chocolate hazelnut spread
400ml/14fl oz/1⅔ cups full cream (whole) milk
90g/3½oz milk chocolate
30ml/2 tbsp extra thick double (heavy) cream (optional)
a little crushed ice
2 chocolate flake bars, to serve

Cook's tip
This drink is extremely rich and filling and should probably be reserved for special occasions, but if you feel that using chocolate flakes as novelty stirrers is a bit too much chocolate for your children, serve the drink with multi-coloured straws or plastic stirrers instead.

1 Put the chocolate spread in a small bowl with 10ml/2 tsp of the milk. Stir well until smooth and glossy.

2 Chop the chocolate. Put 100ml/ 3½fl oz/scant ½ cup of the remaining milk in a small pan and add the chocolate pieces. Heat gently, stirring until the chocolate has dissolved. Remove from the heat and pour into a jug (pitcher). Leave to cool for 10 minutes, then stir in the remaining milk.

3 Using a teaspoon, dot the chocolate hazelnut mixture around the sides of two tall glasses, rotating them so that each glass is randomly streaked with chocolate. Dot the cream around the glasses in the same way, if using.

4 Put a little crushed ice in each glass and pour over the chocolate milk. Serve immediately with flake bar stirrers that can be used to swirl the hazelnut mixture into the chocolate milk.

tempting
dessert
drinks

Irresistible blends that imitate popular desserts are
cleverly transformed into stunning drinks you can
sip leisurely or, in some cases, scoop with a spoon.
Be tempted by true classics such as death by
chocolate and blueberry meringue or, for
something different, try a rhubarb and allspice
cream and an unusual take on banoffee pie.

Frosty fruits

Long after summer is over you can still summon up the glorious flavours of the season by making this fruity and refreshing drink from frozen summer fruits. This purple, slushy, fruity delight will pep up even the darkest mornings. Revitalize yourself with this blend before you leave for work in the morning to give your body a well-deserved boost.

1 Take the frozen fruits straight from the freezer and tip them into a blender or food processor. Blend until finely crushed, scraping down the side of the bowl, if necessary.

2 Add the yogurt and cream to the crushed fruit, then spoon in 30ml/ 2 tbsp of the sugar. Blend again until the mixture is smooth and thick. Taste and add the extra sugar if necessary. Serve immediately, decorated with fruit.

Makes 2–3 glasses

250g/9oz/2 cups frozen summer fruits, plus extra to decorate
200g/7oz/scant 1 cup natural (plain) yogurt
45ml/3 tbsp double (heavy) cream
30–45ml/2–3 tbsp caster (superfine) sugar

Cook's tip
This drink takes only moments to whizz up and you can use any mixture of fruits, whether you've grown your own berries or bought them frozen in bags.

Iced mango lassi

Based on a traditional Indian drink, this is perfect for any occasion: served with spicy food at dinner, at long, hot garden parties, or as a welcome cooler at any time of day. The yogurt ice that forms the basis of this drink is a useful recipe to add to your repertoire because it is much lighter and healthier than classic ice creams.

Makes 3–4 glasses

175g/6oz/scant 1 cup caster (superfine) sugar
150ml/¼ pint/⅔ cup water
2 lemons
500ml/17fl oz/generous 2 cups Greek
　(US strained plain) yogurt
350ml/12fl oz/1½ cups mango juice
ice cubes (optional)
fresh mint sprigs and mango wedges,
　to decorate

1 To make the yogurt ice, put the sugar and water in a saucepan and heat gently, stirring occasionally, until the sugar has dissolved. Pour the syrup into a jug (pitcher). Leave to cool, then chill until very cold.

2 Grate the rind from the lemons and then squeeze out the juice. Add the rind and juice to the chilled syrup and stir well to mix.

3 Pour the syrup mixture into a shallow, freezer container and freeze until thickened. Beat in the yogurt and return to the freezer until the mixture is thick enough to scoop.

4 To serve the drinks, briefly process the mango juice with about ten small scoops of yogurt ice in a blender or food processor until just smooth. Pour equal portions of the mixture into tall glasses or tumblers and add the ice cubes, if using.

5 Top each drink with another scoop of the yogurt ice and decorate with mint sprigs and mango wedges. Serve.

Super sorbet fizz

Freshly blended pineapple and cool, tangy lemon sorbet, topped up with sparkling ginger ale, makes a tastebud-tingling, fantastically mouthwatering drink. This semi-frozen blend is perfect after a summer lunch as a light alternative to more conventional desserts, or as a drink that can be whizzed up to allow you to chill out whenever the mood takes you.

Makes 4 glasses

30ml/2 tbsp muscovado (molasses) sugar
15ml/1 tbsp lemon juice
½ pineapple
1 piece preserved stem ginger,
    roughly chopped
200ml/7fl oz/scant 1 cup lemon sorbet,
    slightly softened
wafer thin pineapple and lemon slices,
    to decorate
ginger ale, to serve

3 Add the sorbet and process briefly until smooth. Spoon the muscovado syrup into four tumblers, then pour in the pineapple mixture.

4 Decorate the edge of the glasses with the pineapple and lemon slices. Top up each glass with ginger ale and serve immediately.

Cook's tip
The easiest way to prepare a pineapple is to chop off the top and base, then slice off the skin. Use the tip of a sharp knife to remove the "eyes" and then roughly chop into chunks.

1 Mix the sugar with the lemon juice in a small bowl and leave to stand for about 5 minutes until it turns syrupy.

2 Discard the skin and core from the pineapple and cut the flesh into chunks. Put the chunks in a blender or food processor with the ginger and whizz until smooth, scraping down the side of the bowl once or twice, if necessary.

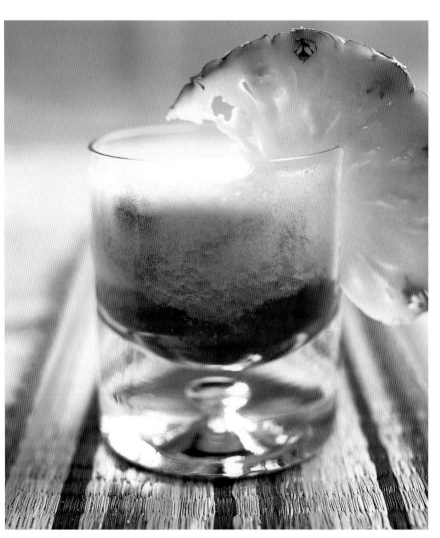

Blueberry meringue crumble

Imagine the most appealing flavours of a blueberry meringue dessert – fresh tangy fruit, crisp sugary meringue and plenty of vanilla-scented cream. This drink combines all of these in one delicious milkshake. Iced yogurt is used to provide a slightly lighter note than ice cream, but there's nothing to stop you using ice cream instead for an even greater indulgence.

1 Put the blueberries and sugar in a blender or food processor with 60ml/ 4 tbsp water and blend until smooth, scraping the mixture down from the side once or twice, if necessary.

2 Transfer the purée to a small bowl and rinse out the blender or food processor bowl to get rid of any remaining blueberry juice.

3 Put the iced yogurt, milk and lime juice in the blender and process until thoroughly combined. Add half of the crushed meringues and process again until smooth.

4 Carefully pour alternate layers of the milkshake, blueberry syrup and the remaining crushed meringues into tall glasses, finishing with a few chunky pieces of meringue.

5 Drizzle any remaining blueberry syrup over the tops of the meringues and decorate with a few extra blueberries. Serve immediately.

Makes 3–4 tall glasses

150g/5oz/1¼ cups fresh blueberries, plus extra to decorate
15ml/1 tbsp icing (confectioners') sugar
250ml/8fl oz/1 cup vanilla iced yogurt
200ml/7fl oz/scant 1 cup full cream (whole) milk
30ml/2 tbsp lime juice
75g/3oz meringues, lightly crushed

Cook's tip
The easiest way to crush the meringues is to put them in a plastic bag on a work surface and tap them gently with a rolling pin. Stop tapping the meringues as soon as they have crumbled into little bitesize pieces otherwise you'll just be left with tiny crumbs.

Rhubarb and allspice cream

Pale shoots of young rhubarb, poached with sugar and spice, and blended with cream, make a truly dreamy concoction. Make this delicious blend early in the season otherwise the rhubarb stalks will be tougher, possibly stringy, and so acidic that you'll need heaps of sugar to make this the indulgent treat that it should be. Serve with a spoon to scoop up every last drop.

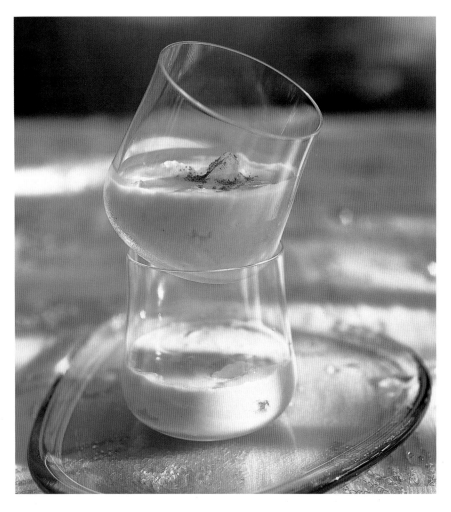

2 Transfer the rhubarb and cooking juice to a blender or food processor and process in short bursts until smooth, scraping down the mixture from the side of the bowl, if necessary.

3 Add the cream and milk to the rhubarb purée and blend again until combined. Transfer to a jug (pitcher) and chill until ready to serve.

4 Half-fill glasses with crushed ice, if using, pour over the juice, sprinkle with allspice and serve immediately.

Cook's tip

If you don't have fresh oranges to squeeze for this drink, you can use orange juice from a carton instead, or try a mix of citrus juices.

Makes 4 glasses

500g/1¼lb early rhubarb
100ml/3½fl oz/scant ½ cup freshly squeezed
   orange juice
75g/3oz/scant ½ cup caster (superfine) sugar
2.5ml/½ tsp ground allspice, plus extra
   to decorate
100ml/3½fl oz/scant ½ cup double
   (heavy) cream
200ml/7fl oz/scant 1 cup full cream
   (whole) milk
crushed ice (optional)

1 Trim the rhubarb and cut it into chunks. Put in a pan with the orange juice, sugar and allspice and bring to the boil. Cover and simmer gently for 6–8 minutes until tender. Remove the pan from the heat and leave to cool.

Turkish delight

If you like Turkish delight, you'll love this fabulously indulgent drink. With the scented aroma of rose water and the delicious icy sweetness of vanilla ice cream, it is difficult to imagine a more decadent, or delicious, combination of ingredients.

Makes 3–4 glasses

125g/4¼oz rose-flavoured Turkish delight
475ml/16fl oz/2 cups semi-skimmed
   (low-fat) milk
250ml/8fl oz/1 cup good quality vanilla
   ice cream
a little finely grated plain (semisweet)
   chocolate, or drinking chocolate powder, for
   sprinkling (optional)

Cook's tips
For an even frothier top on this drink, pour the milkshake into a large bowl and whisk with a hand-held electric mixer.

   If the Turkish delight is very sticky, you'll find it easier to cut it with scissors instead of a knife.

1 Roughly chop the Turkish delight and reserve a few pieces for decoration. Put the rest in a pan with half the milk. Heat gently until the pieces begin to melt. Remove the pan from the heat and leave to cool.

2 Spoon the mixture into a blender or food processor and add the remaining milk. Process until smooth, then add the ice cream and blend briefly to combine. Pour into glasses, top with the reserved Turkish delight and serve, sprinkled with chocolate or drinking chocolate, if using.

Nutty nougat

For the best results, chill this glorious milkshake for a few hours until it is icy cold and the jumble of ingredients has had time to merge into a hedonistic fusion of flavours. Skinning the pistachio nuts is not essential, but it makes a fabulous visual impact, transforming the specks of nut from a dull green to a gorgeous, vivid emerald colour.

Makes 3 glasses

90ml/6 tbsp sweetened condensed milk
300ml/½ pint/1¼ cups semi-skimmed
    (low-fat) milk
100ml/3½fl oz/scant ½ cup crème fraîche
15ml/1 tbsp lemon juice
25g/1oz/¼ cup skinned pistachio nuts
25g/1oz/¼ cup blanched almonds
25g/1oz/3 tbsp candied peel, finely chopped,
    plus a few extra slices for decoration
ice cubes

1 Put the condensed milk and the semi-skimmed milk in a blender or food processor. Add the crème fraîche and blend until combined.

2 Add the lemon juice, pistachio nuts, almonds and chopped peel to the blender or food processor and blend until chopped into tiny pieces. Pour over ice cubes in glasses, add a few slices of candied peel and serve.

Cook's tip

Pretty, emerald-green flecks of pistachio nut pepper this rich, nougat-flavoured milkshake, giving it the subtlest hint of colour and the most wonderful texture.

To skin the pistachio nuts, put them in a heatproof bowl, cover with boiling water and leave for about 2 minutes. Drain the nuts and rub them between layers of kitchen paper to loosen the skins. Pick out the nuts, carefully peeling off the remaining skin.

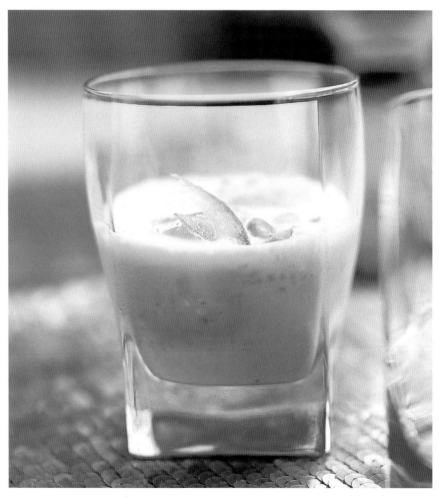

Banoffee high

Make plenty of this outrageous, lip-smacking milkshake because everyone will love it. Nobody is pretending this is a health drink, but it is guaranteed to give you an energy rush of astronomic proportions. Keep any leftover syrup in the refrigerator to use as a quick and delicious toffee sauce for spooning over ice cream.

1 To make the toffee syrup, put the sugar in a small heavy pan with 75ml/5 tbsp water. Heat gently, stirring until the sugar dissolves, then add 45ml/3 tbsp of the cream and bring to the boil. Let the syrup simmer for about 4 minutes until thickened. Remove from the heat and leave to cool for about 30 minutes.

2 Peel the bananas, break into pieces and put into a blender or food processor with the milk, vanilla sugar, ice cubes and a further 45ml/3 tbsp of the cream. Blend until smooth and frothy.

3 Pour the remaining cream into a bowl and whip lightly with a whisk or hand-held electric mixer until it just holds its shape.

4 Add half the toffee syrup to the milkshake and blend, then pour into glasses. Drizzle more syrup around the insides of the glasses. Spoon the whipped cream over and drizzle with any remaining syrup. Serve immediately.

Makes 4 tall glasses

75g/3oz/scant ½ cup light muscovado (brown) sugar
150ml/¼ pint/⅔ cup double (heavy) cream
4 large bananas
600ml/1 pint/2½ cups full cream (whole) milk
15ml/1 tbsp vanilla sugar
8 ice cubes

Cook's tips
If you use a blender, read the instructions to check whether it is powerful enough to cope with crushing ice cubes.
  Make the syrup a little in advance so it has time to thicken.

Coconut and passion fruit ice

Few things beat the unadulterated, pure flavour of freshly juiced coconut. Whizzed with plenty of crushed ice and teamed with sharp, intensely flavoured passion fruit, it produces a milkshake that tastes indulgently good but is still refreshingly natural and wholesome.

Makes 2–3 tall glasses

1 coconut
75ml/5 tbsp icing (confectioners') sugar
3 passion fruit
150g/5oz crushed ice
60ml/4 tbsp double (heavy) cream

Cook's tip

This tropical, icy, passionately luxurious drink is heavenly on a summer's evening. You don't have to be on holiday to enjoy this type of decadence as this drink can be made quickly and easily at any time. Make a jug full and share with friends or family – if you feel that you are able to share it.

1 Drain the milk from the coconut and put to one side. Break open the coconut, remove the flesh, then pare off the brown skin. Push the coconut pieces through a juicer along with 150ml/¼ pint/⅔ cup water. Stir the icing sugar into the juice and reserve.

2 Halve the passion fruit and scoop the pulp into a small bowl. Set aside.

3 Put the crushed ice in a blender or food processor and blend until slushy. Add the juiced coconut, any drained coconut milk and the cream. Process to just blend the ingredients.

4 Pour the mixture into tall stemmed glasses, then, using a teaspoon, spoon the passion fruit on top of the drink. Add stirrers, if you like, and serve.

Death by chocolate

There are only two ingredients used in this decadently rich smoothie: creamy milk and the best chocolate you can buy. Blended together, they make the frothiest, smoothest and most deliciously chocolatey drink you will ever taste. Once you've tried this recipe, you will never view a chocolate smoothie in the same light again.

Makes 2 large glasses

150g/5oz good quality chocolate
350ml/12fl oz/1½ cups full cream
    (whole) milk
ice cubes
chocolate curls or shavings, to serve

Cook's tip

Depending on personal taste, use dark (bittersweet) chocolate with 70 per cent cocoa solids, or a good quality milk chocolate. If you like the intensity of dark chocolate but the creaminess of milk, try using half of each type.

1 Break the chocolate into pieces and place in a heatproof bowl set over a pan of simmering water, making sure that the bowl does not rest in the water.

2 Add 60ml/4 tbsp of the milk and leave until the chocolate melts, stirring occasionally with a wooden spoon.

3 Remove the bowl from the heat, pour the remaining milk over the chocolate and stir to combine.

4 Pour the mixture into a blender or food processor and blend until frothy. Pour into glasses, add ice and chocolate curls or shavings, then serve.

Coffee frappé

This creamy, smooth creation, which is strictly for adults (because of the alcoholic content), makes a wonderful alternative to a dessert on a hot summer's evening – or indeed at any time when you feel you need to indulge yourself. Serve in small glasses or little cappuccino cups for a glamorous touch, and provide your guests with both straws and long-handled spoons to allow them to scoop out every last bit of this delicious drink.

Makes 4 glasses

8 scoops of classic coffee ice cream
90ml/6 tbsp Kahlúa or Tia Maria liqueur
150ml/¼ pint/⅔ cup single (light) cream
1.5ml/¼ tsp ground cinnamon (optional)
crushed ice
ground cinnamon, for sprinkling

Cook's tip
To make a non-alcoholic version of this drink, simply substitute strong black coffee for the Kahlúa or Tia Maria.

1 Put half the coffee ice cream in a food processor or blender. Add the liqueur, then pour in the cream with a little cinnamon, if using, and blend. Scoop the remaining ice cream into four glasses or cappuccino cups.

2 Using a dessertspoon, spoon the coffee cream over the ice cream in each glass, then top with a little crushed ice. Sprinkle the top of each frappé with a little ground cinnamon and serve immediately.

Cool chocolate float

Frothy, chocolatey milkshake and scoops of creamy sweet chocolate and vanilla ice cream are combined here to make the most meltingly delicious drink ever, which is sure to prove a big success with children and adults alike. If you simply adore chocolate and you love ice cream, this may be the perfect drink for you. As this is such a rich, indulgent blend, however, try and resist temptation and don't indulge too often – save it for very special occasions.

Makes 2 tall glasses

115g/4oz plain (semisweet) chocolate, broken
  into pieces
250ml/8fl oz/1 cup milk
15ml/1 tbsp caster (superfine) sugar
4 large scoops of classic vanilla ice cream
4 large scoops of dark (bittersweet) chocolate
  ice cream
a little lightly whipped cream
grated chocolate or chocolate curls,
  to decorate

Cook's tip
Try substituting banana, coconut or toffee ice cream for the chocolate and vanilla ice cream if you prefer.

1 Put the chocolate in a heavy pan and add the milk and sugar. Heat gently, stirring with a wooden spoon until the chocolate has melted and the mixture is smooth. Leave to cool.

2 Blend the cooled chocolate mixture with half of the ice cream in a blender or food processor.

3 Scoop the remaining ice cream alternately into two tall glasses: vanilla then chocolate. Using a dessertspoon, drizzle the chocolate milk over and around the ice cream in each glass. Top with lightly whipped cream and sprinkle over a little grated chocolate or some chocolate curls to decorate. Serve immediately.

Rum and raisin thick-shake

This rich and creamy milkshake, based on the classic combination of rum and raisins, is remarkably easy to prepare. Use a good quality ice cream, leave it to soften slightly in the refrigerator before scooping, and you simply can't go wrong. If the raisins are a little dry, leave them to soak in the rum for a few minutes to soften and plump up before you blend them.

1 Put the raisins, rum and a little of the milk into a blender or food processor and process for about 1 minute, or until the raisins are finely chopped.

2 Spoon two large scoops of the vanilla ice cream into two tall glasses and put the remaining ice cream and milk into the blender. Process until creamy.

3 Pour the milkshake into glasses and serve immediately with straws and long spoons for scooping up the raisins.

Makes 2 tall glasses

75g/3oz/generous ½ cup raisins
45ml/3 tbsp dark rum
300ml/½ pint/1¼ cups full cream
(whole) milk
500ml/17fl oz/2¼ cups good quality vanilla
ice cream

Cook's tip
As an alternative, replace the vanilla ice cream with a good quality chocolate-flavoured ice cream – this will taste exceptionally good with rum and raisins.

Espresso crush

A fresh update on iced coffee, this creatively layered treat combines slushy frozen granita with a thick vanilla ice cream layer, and is perfect for rounding off a lazy summer lunch or as a late afternoon refresher. The granita needs several hours in the freezer but will then keep for weeks so it is ready and waiting whenever you fancy a burst of ice-cold espresso.

Makes 4 glasses

75ml/5 tbsp ground espresso coffee
75g/3oz/scant ½ cup caster (superfine) sugar
300g/11oz vanilla ice cream or
   vanilla iced non-dairy dessert
75ml/5 tbsp milk or soya milk

1 Put the coffee in a cafetière (press pot), add 750ml/1¼ pints/3 cups boiling water and leave to infuse for 5 minutes. Plunge the cafetière and pour the coffee into a shallow freezer container. Stir in the sugar until dissolved. Leave to cool completely, then cover and freeze for about 2 hours or until the mixture starts to turn slushy around the edges.

2 Using a fork, break up the ice crystals, stirring them into the centre of the container. Re-freeze until the mixture is slushy around the edges again. Repeat forking and stirring once or twice more until the mixture is completely slushy and there is no liquid remaining. Re-freeze until ready to use.

Cook's tip
The softened ice cream will melt quickly once you start layering it up in the glasses, so a good trick is to thoroughly chill the glasses before using them.

3 Put the ice cream or iced dessert and milk in a blender or food processor and process until thick and smooth. To serve, spoon a little into the base of each glass and sprinkle with a layer of the granita. Repeat layering until the glasses are full. Serve immediately.

White chocolate and hazelnut cream

This luxurious combination of smooth, creamy white chocolate and crunchy hazelnut is simply irresistible. To get the maximum flavour from the hazelnuts, it is always best to use whole ones, toasting them first to develop their nuttiness and then grinding them fresh, rather than using ready chopped or ground nuts.

Makes 3 glasses

90g/3½oz/scant 1 cup blanched hazelnuts
150g/5oz white chocolate
300ml/½ pint/1¼ cups full cream
   (whole) milk
4 large scoops white chocolate or vanilla
   ice cream
a little freshly grated nutmeg (optional)

1 Roughly chop the hazelnuts using a large, sharp knife, then toast them lightly in a dry frying pan, turning continuously to ensure that they are toasted evenly. Reserve 30ml/2 tbsp for decoration, then tip the remainder into a blender or food processor. Blend until very finely ground.

2 Finely chop the chocolate and reserve 30ml/2 tbsp for decoration. Put the remainder in a small, heavy pan with half of the milk and heat very gently until the chocolate has melted thoroughly. Stir until smooth, then pour the chocolate into a bowl. Add the remaining milk, stir and leave to cool.

3 Add the melted chocolate mixture to the blender with the ice cream and a little grated nutmeg, if using. Blend until the mixture is smooth. Pour into glasses and sprinkle with the reserved hazelnuts and chocolate. Grate over a little extra nutmeg, if you like, and serve immediately.

Ice cool coconut

This fabulously cooling, dairy-free drink is just about as silky smooth as they come. Rather than using coconut milk, this recipe opts for desiccated coconut, steeped in water, which is then strained to extract the flavour. Without the nutty texture, this delicious coconut feast slides down very nicely on a summer's evening. If it's the weekend – or even if it's not – and you fancy a bit of a treat, add a splash of Malibu or coconut-flavoured liqueur.

Makes 2–3 glasses

150g/5oz/2½ cups desiccated (dry
   unsweetened shredded) coconut
30ml/2 tbsp lime juice
30ml/2 tbsp icing (confectioners') sugar, plus
   extra for dusting
200g/7oz vanilla iced non-dairy dessert
lime slices, to decorate

Cook's tip
Desiccated coconut can be bought ready sweetened. If using this, you may wish to omit the sugar that's added with the lime juice.

1 Put the coconut in a heatproof bowl and add 600ml/1 pint/2½ cups boiling water. Leave to stand for 30 minutes. Strain the coconut through a sieve lined with muslin (cheesecloth) into a bowl, pressing the pulp with a spoon to extract as much juice as possible. Discard the pulp and chill the coconut milk.

2 Pour the coconut milk into a blender or food processor with the lime juice, sugar and non-dairy dessert. Blend thoroughly until completely smooth. Pour into glasses and decorate with lime slices. Lightly dust the lime slices and edges of the glasses with icing sugar and serve immediately.

real
boozy
blends

If you're entertaining friends or simply relaxing
after a hard day's work, try one of these
tasty tipples, which are guaranteed to put
everyone in a mellow mood. Some are fruity and
only mildly alcoholic, while others are spirit-based
and pack a real punch – there's something
here to suit every occasion.

Iced strawberry daiquiri

The classic daiquiri cocktail is named after a village in Cuba that lies near the Bacardi processing plant. The original version was an incredibly potent blend of rum and whisky but the fruit versions, which are so popular today, are slightly less alcoholic. This one combines sweet and fragrant strawberries with white rum and refreshingly tangy lime juice.

Makes 4 small glasses

4 limes
60ml/4 tbsp icing (confectioners') sugar
200ml/7fl oz/scant 1 cup white rum
275g/10oz/2½ cups strawberries
300g/11oz crushed ice

Cook's tip
To make a really slushy, thick iced daiquiri, use frozen strawberries. There's no need to leave them to thaw, just use them as they are.

To make a banana version of this drink, replace the strawberries with two bananas. Peel the bananas, break them into pieces and add with the rum and icing sugar.

1 Squeeze the limes and pour the juice into a blender or food processor. Add the icing sugar, rum and all but two of the strawberries. Process until really smooth and frothy.

2 Add the crushed ice to the blender or food processor and blend until slushy. Pour the daiquiri into glasses, add a strawberry half to each glass and serve.

Frozen margarita

For the serious cocktail connoisseur, a margarita sipped with a slice of lime from the salt-crusted rim of a glass is simply the best choice. A classic citrus juicer will help you to get the maximum juice from limes, but if the fruits are very firm and don't yield much juice, you could try giving them a brief blast in the microwave first.

1 To coat the glass rims with salt, put 30ml/2 tbsp of the lime juice into a saucer and plenty of salt flakes in another. Turn the glasses upside down and dip the rim of each glass in the lime juice, then in the salt. Invert the glasses again and put to one side.

2 Put the remaining lime juice in a blender or food processor with the Cointreau or Grand Marnier, tequila and ice. Process until the mixture is slushy.

3 Pour the margarita mixture into the salt-rimmed glasses, add a slice of lime to each glass and serve immediately.

Makes 8 small glasses

150ml/¼ pint/⅔ cup lime juice, from about
   6 large limes
sea salt flakes
120ml/4fl oz/½ cup Cointreau or
   Grand Marnier
200ml/7fl oz/scant 1 cup tequila
150g/5oz crushed ice
1 lime, thinly sliced, to decorate

Cook's tip
Gold tequila has aged in casks for longer than white and has a slightly golden tinge to it. Try to use clear tequila for this recipe as it will result in a fresh, clear cocktail in which the colour of the lime really shows through.

Mint julep

Traditionally, a julep is a sweetened, iced drink made using brandy or whisky and flavoured with fresh mint leaves. This stunning version infuses the mint in sugar syrup to colour it a cooling shade of green. Zipped up with brandy, or delicious peach brandy, and poured over ice, this makes a refreshingly good summertime tipple.

Makes 4 small glasses

25g/1oz/2 tbsp caster (superfine) sugar
25g/1oz fresh mint, plus extra mint sprigs, to decorate
crushed ice
100ml/7 tbsp brandy or peach brandy

Cook's tip
This sexy little number would be well placed in any cosmopolitan New York cocktail bar. To bring a little bit of that New York ambience into your home, prepare a large batch and invite plenty of friends round to help you drink it.

1 Put the sugar in a small, heavy pan with 200ml/7fl oz/scant 1 cup water. Heat gently until the sugar dissolves, then bring to the boil and boil for 1 minute to make a syrup. Pour into a small bowl. Pull the mint leaves from the stalks and add to the hot syrup. Leave the syrup to stand for about 30 minutes or until cool.

2 Strain the syrup into a blender or food processor, add the mint and blend lightly until it is finely chopped.

3 Half-fill four small glasses with crushed ice, packing one or two mint sprigs into each glass. Mix the brandy with the mint syrup and pour over the ice. Serve immediately.

Lime mojito

Cuba and the Caribbean islands have invented some of the most delicious lime- and rum-based cocktails, from tangily refreshing shorts to thick, creamy concoctions that are almost a meal in themselves. This recipes fits the first category, but beware, you're bound to find it irresistibly moreish – which could prove dangerous.

Makes 4 glasses

4 lemon balm sprigs
40ml/8 tsp caster (superfine) sugar
4 limes
130ml/4½fl oz/generous ½ cup white rum
ice cubes
strips of pared lime rind, to decorate
sparkling mineral water, to serve

Cook's tip
To ensure you get the maximum juice from the limes, microwave them for approximately 20–30 seconds on medium (50 per cent power).

1 Pull the lemon balm leaves from their stems. Put 10ml/2 tsp of the sugar into each small glass.

2 Add several lemon balm leaves to each glass and lightly rub the leaves into the sugar, using the back of a teaspoon, to release their fragrance.

3 Squeeze the limes using a citrus juicer, or by hand, and then pour the juice into the glasses with the rum.

4 Add plenty of ice to each glass and decorate with pared lime rind. Serve immediately, topped up with sparkling mineral water.

Tropical fruit royale

This recipe is a fresh and fruity variation of a kir royale, in which Champagne is poured over crème de cassis. Made with tropical fruits and sparkling wine, this cocktail is a lot less expensive than the Champagne version but still has a wonderfully elegant feel. Remember to blend the fruits ahead of time to give the mango ice cubes time to freeze.

Makes 6 glasses

2 large mangoes
6 passion fruit
sparkling wine

Cook's tip
Delight your guests with this delicious thirst-quencher. With its taste of the tropics, it makes the perfect choice for garden parties on balmy summer evenings, wherever in the world you are.

1 Peel the mangoes, cut the flesh off the stone (pit), then put the flesh in a blender or food processor. Process until smooth, scraping the mixture down from the side of the bowl, if necessary.

2 Fill an ice-cube tray with half of the purée and freeze for 2 hours.

3 Cut six wedges from one or two of the passion fruit and scoop the pulp from the rest of the passion fruit into the remaining mango purée. Process until well blended.

4 Spoon the mixture into six stemmed glasses. Divide the mango ice cubes among the glasses, top up with sparkling wine and add the passion fruit wedges. Serve with stirrers, if you like.

Pineapple and coconut rum crush

This thick and slushy tropical cooler is unbelievably rich thanks to the combination of coconut milk and thick cream. The addition of sweet, juicy and slightly tart pineapple, and finely crushed ice, offers a refreshing foil, making it all too easy to sip your way through several glasses.

1 Trim off the ends from the pineapple, then cut off the skin. Cut away the core and chop the flesh. Put the chopped flesh in a blender or food processor with the lemon juice and whizz until very smooth.

2 Add the coconut milk, cream, rum and 30ml/2 tbsp of the sugar. Blend until thoroughly combined, then taste and add more sugar if necessary. Pack the ice into glasses and pour the drink over. Serve immediately.

Makes 4–5 large glasses

1 pineapple
30ml/2 tbsp lemon juice
200ml/7fl oz/scant 1 cup coconut milk
150ml/¼ pint/⅔ cup double (heavy) cream
200ml/7fl oz/scant 1 cup white rum
30–60ml/2–4 tbsp caster (superfine) sugar
500g/1¼lb finely crushed ice

Cook's tip
This is a great cocktail for making ahead of time. Blend the drink in advance and chill in a jug (pitcher). Store the crushed ice in the freezer ready for serving as soon as it's required.

Foaming citrus eggnog

For most of us, eggnog is inextricably associated with the festive season. This version, however, pepped up with orange rind and juice for a lighter, fresher taste, has a much wider appeal. Whether you sip it as a late-night soother, serve it as a wintry dessert or enjoy it as a cosy tipple on a wet afternoon, it's sure to bring a warm, rosy glow to your cheeks.

Makes 2 glasses

2 small oranges
150ml/¼ pint/⅔ cup single (light) cream
plenty of freshly grated nutmeg
2.5ml/½ tsp ground cinnamon
2.5ml/½ tsp cornflour (cornstarch)
2 eggs, separated
30ml/2 tbsp light muscovado (brown) sugar
45ml/3 tbsp brandy
extra nutmeg, for sprinkling (optional)

1 Finely grate the rind from the oranges, then squeeze out the juice and pour it into a jug (pitcher).

2 Put the rind in a small heavy pan with the cream, nutmeg, cinnamon and cornflour. Heat gently over a low heat, stirring frequently until bubbling.

3 Whisk the egg yolks with the sugar, using a handheld whisk.

4 Stir the hot citrus cream mixture into the egg yolks, then return to the pan. Pour in the orange juice and brandy and heat very gently, stirring until slightly thickened.

5 Whisk the egg whites in a large, clean bowl until foamy and light.

6 Strain the cream mixture through a sieve into the whisked whites. Stir gently and pour into heatproof punch cups, handled glasses or mugs. Sprinkle over a little extra nutmeg before serving, if you like.

Cook's tip
Note that this recipe contains almost raw egg.

Amaretto apricot dream

This really is a dream of a drink, combining fresh, ripe apricots, oranges and delicious maple syrup with creamy cool yogurt. Light and fruity, it is a wonderful choice for a breezy, sunny day in the garden, and the addition of almond liqueur and amaretti biscuits gives it a wonderfully complex flavour. Once you've tasted one you'll surely be back for more.

Makes 4 glasses

3 large oranges
600g/1lb 6oz small fresh apricots
60ml/4 tbsp maple syrup, plus extra
   to serve
50g/2oz amaretti
200g/7oz/scant 1 cup Greek (strained
   plain) yogurt
30ml/2 tbsp amaretto liqueur
mineral water (optional)
ice cubes

1 Grate the rind from one of the oranges and squeeze the juice from all three. Halve and stone (pit) the apricots and put them in a pan. Add the orange juice and zest then heat slowly. Cover with a lid and simmer very gently for 3 minutes or until the apricots are tender. Strain through a sieve, reserving the juice, and leave to cool completely.

2 Put half the fruit, the strained juice, maple syrup and amaretti in a food processor or blender and blend until smooth. Arrange the remaining fruit halves in the bases of four glasses.

3 Stir the yogurt until smooth and spoon half over the fruits. Add the amaretto, and a little mineral water to the blended mixture (if the juice is too thick), and pour into the glasses. Add the remaining yogurt and one or two ice cubes to each glass. Drizzle with maple syrup to serve.

Cook's tip
To impress guests at parties, use two teaspoons to delicately place a spoonful of yogurt on top of this apricot drink.

index